TRANSACTIONS
of the
Society of Fellows
of Dyson College

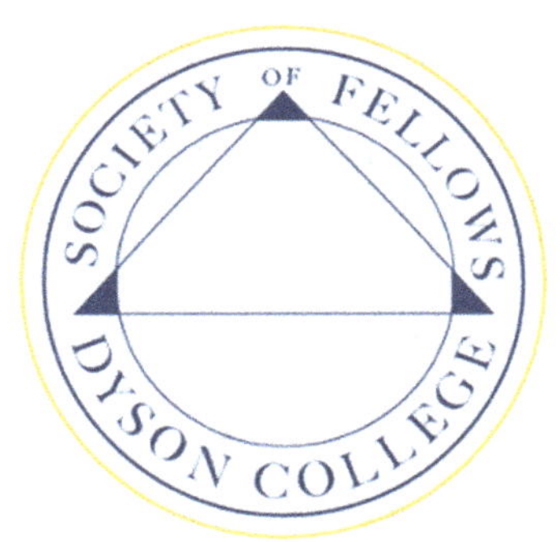

Volume 25
2025

Publication: Transactions, Volume 25, 2025

Editor: Judith Pajo

Faculty Board: Zafir Buraei; Ramón Emilio Fernández; Paul Griffin; Kier Hanratty; Brandyn Heppard; Stephanie Hsu; Maria Iacullo-Bird; Mary Kaltenberg; Sergey Kazakov; Jillian McDonald; Rita Upmacis; Mark Weinstock; Melvin Williams

Additional Reviewers: Erika Crispo

Editorial Address: Society of Fellows
                        Dyson College of Arts and Sciences
                        Pace University
                        41 Park Row, Room 717
                        New York, NY 10038

Email Address: sof@pace.edu

Published by: Society of Fellows of Dyson College

Printed by: Pace University Press

Designed by: Zetta Whiting and Kayleigh Woltal

ISBN: 978-1-965246-02-3

The editors and faculty board of the Society of Fellows welcome comments on articles that have appeared in Transactions of the Society of Fellows of Dyson College.

DYSON COLLEGE OF ARTS AND SCIENCES

The Dyson College of Arts and Sciences offers a robust and innovative liberal arts education distinguished by its emphasis on faculty mentoring, experiential learning, and small classes. Through instruction in over fifty majors and minors across the disciplines of the arts and sciences, Dyson College prepares its students for graduate and professional schools, and the twenty-first century workforce. Students develop their potential for achievement through both academic and co-curricular programs and activities, and outstanding among these is the Society of Fellows of Dyson College.

SOCIETY OF FELLOWS OF DYSON COLLEGE

HISTORY

The Society of Fellows began in the fall of 1980 with a weekend seminar devoted to questions in applied ethics. The first class of members inducted at the formal inauguration of the society in December 1981 was named after distinguished philosopher and Pace faculty member William Barrett. Since then, a new class is inducted annually and named after a fellow who has made a significant contribution to the ideals of the Society of Fellows. To date, more than 700 students, faculty, and alumni hold the distinction of being a fellow, and the Society of Fellows has become the premier honors organization in Dyson College.

FOUNDING CHARTER

Charles H. Dyson, Edward J. Mortola, Joseph E. Houle, M. Teresa Brady, R.D.C, John H. Buchsbaum, Louis V. Quintas

Being bound by ties of friendship and dedication to the ideals of liberal education, do hereby constitute themselves and their successors, forever, as fellows of the Dyson College with the duty of promoting undergraduate scholarship among the members of said college and admitting into its society and fellowship only those students, faculty, alumni, staff and friends of the Dyson College who advance in a noteworthy and exemplary fashion the purposes of the society as expressed in its constitution.

MEMBERSHIP

Membership is open to students, faculty, and alumni of Dyson College who meet eligibility requirements and contribute to the goals of the Society of Fellows.

Enrolled students of Pace University who demonstrate excellence in scholarship or in artistic creativity will be invited to become fellows if they meet the following criteria:

1. Minimum 3.3 QPA (cumulative quality point average); exceptions will be considered on a case-by-case basis.

2. Participation in at least two Society of Fellows-sponsored events; one of these events must be presentation of research or artistic projects at the annual meeting.

3. Submission of an outstanding signature work of scholarship or creative expression; to fulfill this requirement, the candidate may use a full-length paper or artistic project submitted for the annual meeting.

4. Letter of recommendation from a faculty member attesting in detail to the quality of the academic work and achievements that are being submitted for the candidate's advancement to fellow.

5. Attendance at the initiation ceremony held annually during the spring semester.

All completed applications meeting eligibility requirements will be reviewed and voted on by the Faculty Executive Board of the Society of Fellows of Dyson College.

Faculty qualify to become fellows when they serve two or more times as mentors of research papers or artistic projects presented at the annual meeting. Faculty also are recognized for sponsoring student works accepted for publication in Transactions, and for serving as weekend seminar leaders. Faculty and alumni of Dyson College who share and further the aims of the society in other outstanding ways also may become fellows.

ACTIVITIES

The annual signature activities of the fellows are the weekend seminar, the annual meeting, and the initiation ceremony. The weekend seminar provides opportunities for students, faculty, and alumni to discuss issues of contemporary significance under the leadership of teacher-scholars. The annual meeting is a one-day student conference where undergraduate students present their research or artistic projects completed under the supervision of faculty mentors. The event also is open to graduate students, several of whom annually apply to participate. At the initiation ceremony, qualified applicants are recognized as fulfilling the eligibility criteria and are inducted as fellows. Transactions of the Society of Fellows of Dyson College is the official journal of the society. Peer-reviewed by Dyson faculty, the journal publishes the work of Pace University undergraduate students completed under the sponsorship of faculty, who often are fellows.

GOVERNANCE

A faculty executive board that reports to the Dyson College dean governs the Society of Fellows of Dyson College. The board facilitates the achievement of the society's goals by planning activities, organizing seminars, reviewing papers, and overseeing special recognitions and awards.

INFORMATION FOR TRANSACTIONS CONTRIBUTORS

Papers published in Transactions are the work of Pace University undergraduate students under the sponsorship of Dyson College faculty members or faculty fellows of the society. Student submissions originate as faculty-sponsored papers or artistic projects that have been presented at an annual meeting of the society. Recent alumni of Dyson College also may submit a paper or a revision of a paper that was presented at an annual meeting. The call for proposals for submission to Transactions is announced in the spring at the annual meeting. Papers or correspondence may be submitted at that time to the editor by email to sof@pace.edu. Each submission will be refereed and considered for inclusion by the editor and associate editors. Papers must be submitted as a Microsoft Word document using 12-point font and double-spaced, with a maximum length of twenty pages. The citation style of a submission's discipline must be followed with respect to footnotes, endnotes, and works cited. For general guidance on the preparation of submissions, consult the Society of Fellows pages on the Pace website.

Judith Pajo, Ph.D.
Associate Professor of Anthropology
Chair of Society of Fellows
Dyson College of Arts and Sciences
Pace University
jpajo@pace.edu

FROM THE EDITOR

Throughout 2024, Pace students involved in the Society of Fellows dedicated considerable effort to original research and creative projects that resonate with our current times. While some worked in libraries and archives, others worked in laboratories or the field, all collaborating with devoted Dyson faculty who mentored undergraduate researchers, guiding them toward the more significant questions facing humanity.

During the spring semester, committed students shared their work with a broader audience, including faculty, students, alumni, friends, family, and Pace's neighbors at the Annual Meeting in New York City. In the fall semester, student and faculty fellows, along with others interested in becoming fellows of the society, gathered for the Weekend Seminar, "Transgression as Power: Breaking the Rules for Change." This thought (and action)-provoking seminar, led by Marcella Szablewicz, PhD (Communication and Media Studies, New York), Ying Wang, PhD (Modern Languages and Cultures, New York), and R. Emilio Fernández, PhD (Mathematics, Westchester), was hosted at a new location just an hour's drive from New York City in Stony Point, NY, on the Hudson River. Participants spent the entire weekend discussing scholarly engagements with the concept of transgression in the many different fields covered by Dyson faculty and students who contributed to the interdisciplinary seminar.

This new issue of Transactions highlights the exceptional work of just a few undergraduate students engaged in the Society of Fellows at Dyson College. It features three articles in the humanities, three in the sciences, and two in the social sciences, selected from over 60 student papers and presentations submitted for review by fellows in the society last year. In the humanities, students in this issue explore essential aspects of the human experience by reflecting on literary works and, in one case, writing their own poems. This work is invaluable for future scholars seeking insight into how the current generation perceives itself and the world. The focus on fluidity over binaries across all three contributions illustrates the ongoing movement toward breaking rules for change, as reflected in our recent seminar. In the natural sciences, students investigated biological and chemical systems to benefit human health and the planet's well-being; climate change, for instance, remains a significant concern for our student researchers. We greatly appreciate the detailed descriptions of the experimental designs in these articles. In the social sciences, students employed statistical analysis and comparative designs across different regions and periods; disparities continue to draw students' attention. Once again, we value the care taken to detail the methods of analysis. Overall, we are impressed by the scientific rigor of these contributions.

What is missing in this issue? How can we account for the lack of contributions in the qualitative tradition of the social sciences? Perhaps those students spent less time at their desks and more time in the field this past year, participating in and observing various social movements that characterize the current historical moment? So much is happening that needs to be documented in real-time and understood. However, gaining this understanding requires time, especially as the subjects and categories evolve. We should anticipate the future contributions of this particular group of student researchers as they begin to make sense of the current social transformations.

Finally, we extend our sincere gratitude to the Society of Fellows faculty board for their efforts in reviewing abstracts and papers for the Annual Meeting and, once again, for their inclusion in this issue of Transactions. Additionally, we express our appreciation to our other reviewers for Transactions. We are particularly grateful to the faculty mentors who dedicated their time year-round to guide our ambitious undergraduate students throughout their research endeavors and who played significant roles as poster judges, panel moderators, and roundtable discussants at the Annual Meeting, as well as co-leaders and guest speakers at the Weekend Seminar. Furthermore, we are pleased to acknowledge Ankita Thakkar and Priyank Sakpal, two graduate students who are recent additions to the SOF team that works behind the scenes to ensure our events run smoothly, as well as Zetta Whiting, another graduate student, for implementing the design and layout of this issue of Transactions. Our deepest thanks go to Dean Tresmaine Grimes and Associate Dean Charlotte Becket for their unwavering support of Transactions and the Society of Fellows. Thank you all!

Judith Pajo, Ph.D.

January 2025

FINE ARTS & HUMANITIES

Bedtime Stories from Brooklyn
By **Felicity Flores**
Sponsored by **Eugene Richie, Ph.D.**
English Language and Literature, New York

From excommunication to the exhilaration of Queer spirituality.

THE COLOR PINK

i think it makes god smile that i live in the color pink

i absconded from the catholic church

still wearing the color i was swaddled in for my christening

i bet it makes god smile that i didn't forget about them entirely

before i developed this slingshot mouth of mine

i was a kid with incessant questions, pen in my pocketbook

the catholic church doesn't care for kids slack-jawed staring at the sky

they could grow into Gailelo willing to live and die for something other than their god

the church tells us there is no life worth living after ex-communication

before i gave up on god entirely

in sunday school it rained like god lost their temper

"i don't understand why god's a man, shouldn't he be more, something we don't yet understand?"

"the reason god is a man—is that men are the ones who tell us what we should see.

if women held power god would be woman.

it's not about what we see, it's about who we talk to when there's trouble–" Mr. Ward tells me

sunday school teacher by day, scientist in the evening, a magician by trade,

he doesn't look at me like i've lost my mind

i think it makes god smile that i live in the color pink

i've been dreaming of running from my mother for as long as i can remember

but i still call, i never stop looking for her love in Basilicas

i bet she thinks i lost my mind this time

before i could hold the language i knew i was different

adults chuckled, my mother turned pink, i frowned

"you're a girl you have to sit with your knees together" the choir sang

"i'm not a girl, i'm Roxaileen!"

"the child's just confused" adults assuaged

i think it makes god smile that i live in the color pink

my mother cites my favorite color as why this gender nonsense makes no goddamn sense

i gesture towards my childhood comics and the closet full of button-downs

i wore a wife pleaser under all my polyester polos to make everything flatter, firmer, sharper

spent an adolescence yearning to be taller and broader

my mother pulls out a pink tulle skirt and i look away

i think it makes god smile that i live in the color pink

i tried to love green the sage silk kiss, lime green iphone of the 2010s, suburban greenery

i tried to love red in all her depths of crimson, studies in scarlett, redhead temptresses

i tried to love blue the gentle touch of azure, the cobalt blue quickness, electric blue voices

i fell in love with someone like me who's lilac, touches like indigo, knows why i turn periwinkle

but, i've always been pink

i've always been blush easy to love, too roguish of a rogue difficult to understand

i've always been bubblegum something you can't swallow
i've always been magnetic magenta an eternal magnum opus

i think it makes god smile that i live in the color pink
something for old time's sake
something god recognizes gifting to me
maybe i can't give up on God
because there's pink
in all this ugliness
rampant violent ugliness against everything i am
there's pink
when i loved pink as fact
ignored God as fiction
interrogated God on gender
i realized if God has no gender i am in their image
i could be pink-face flushed
and still keep my name
a name gifted to me melded of two words for my namesake to have and
to hold
because i could never just belong to one

A tale of true love in the age of the pandemic.

LIPSTICK STAIN ON MY MASK

the plague could have taken you from me

i prayed to spoon feed you blueberry oatmeal when we became more bone than body

for your vaccination you put down my dorm address

slipped a note to the practitioner that if your mother knew you were vaccinated she would keep your house keys indefinitely

i wore a low cut top as ample distraction when the needle went into your arm

you shut your eyes and held my hand

buried your face in my neck after

you've always had a deadly fear of needles

i admit i am afraid of losing you

i confess as long as i have loved you i've always been afraid

one day your mother would hit you too hard then you'd fall into the blunt edge of the coffee table that so proudly displays your sister's awards

one day you'd be crossing through an alley at an inopportune time then men who had tequila for dinner and cruelty in their hearts would harm you

one day someone whose mind escaped them would open their car door,

as you were biking past

i was most afraid that the plague could have taken you from me

in the infinite kindness of a higher power

i love you enough to cheat death, you love me enough to double cross the life you were born into, i love you in the lives that we were separated too soon

i love in every ailment and absence of health

Kindred spirits from the age of slumber parties into adulthood.

BEJEWELED (PRETTY LITTLE FOOL)

when we were kids i probably told you
"if i have a daughter i hope she's a pretty little fool"
drowning in my defiance and dramatics

you probably told me
i would be a wonderful mother
(i would have agreed to end the conversation)

pride is an ugly thing we adorn ourselves in
you know my vanity is reserved for my work
you know i have to need no play house
to mother, to coddle, to love unprovoked

resentment is an ugly thing we adorn ourselves in
at sixteen i shoved a chain in your palm
told you promises are reserved for fools
you know i needed you
i know i could've trusted your judgment

diamonds are a girl's best friend
i wear your sardonyx
you wear my emeralds

when we first met i told you i loved your earrings
years later vowed to your mother i'd buy your daughter a pair of her
own
i will
your daughter will know who you were before her
i will smudge out the lipstick stains i placed on her cheeks
tell her about her sage mother and her emeralds

Brooklyn neighborhoods hold intergenerational conversations of first loves and losses.

WELCOME TO ROME (NEW HOME, SAME HEADRUSH)

all roads lead to rome, west side story, last loves in canarsie

i've used a clever idiom or two to describe loving you

i collect clichés, stuff them in my pocketbook, kiss you as a way to reapply your lipstick

you grew up alone with your encyclopedia and your echolalia drove your teachers insane

schoolyard bullies outed you, your mother shrieked, fox news continued business as usual

swore you were unlovable, though birds flocked to you, stayed perched on your shoulder

you cried when the woodpecker died on your swing

i cried when my aunts left BedStuy

that apartment was the only calm i knew

i played chess alone, they called me a faggot, i stopped writing the poem

i didn't realize that other girls didn't have raven-haired, smoke-show-singers on their ceilings

i raised my brother with thomas the train, relived my boyhood through his

i was academically exceptional, "black girls speak when spoken to"

swore i'd never marry, privately longing for someone to stand on the outside of the sidewalk

you've become such a sentimental darling, you archive our lives

you pout to save the charred headscarf beyond redemption from the dryer revel in my pink lint from the dryer, i live in your monochromes of lavender

your mother had forbidden you to set foot in the train station, even so you waited three hours for me at huntington

cheated fate, electromagnetic spectrum, all roads lead to rome

An ode to James Baldwin from one oldest child to another.

HONEY IN THE HIVE

Mr. Baldwin you've buried your younger brothers before you

i am the oldest son and i too am afraid

i fear my mother thinks i poisoned the ink well my brother sketches from

i didn't raise him to be prismatic like me

in my pragmatic nature i assure you i wanted to protect him

i wished for him to understand the grand expansive nature

my brother isn't a cherry pie boy

he's a peach pie darling

i fear for his life

you remember signing your name for your friend Mr. and Mrs. Evers

only to never see his smile again, to hear of his last breath taken over the radio

i imagine that suddenly the songbird in you fell silent

it stopped raining in London

when your sister Gloria put down her fork to tell you Malcolm X had died

i imagine that you couldn't eat that kind of chicken ever again

when you danced with Lorraine Hansbury you knew she was a force of nature

Lorraine Hansbury had no intention to beguile when she sent a look of lightning at bobby kennedy

i imagine that when she left this rock the wind in Paris died

Mr. Baldwin i am afraid my baby brother will one day bury me earlier than he could anticipate

perhaps because i too could not remain in Paris to discuss the Black american issue from my sunlit desk

i have never been able to shut my mouth

i have never had the self preservation to roll over and play dead

i would have died amongst your brother in the 60s

i am too fearful to live in my 20s
yet i am so willing to lay down my life
in exchange for my brother's future
is this futile¿

i am trapped within the land of the living and where only death can
reach
you knew the ammunition in your pen
you saw the Black children arms outstretched for your words
yet you remembered Ms. Miller, the white schoolteacher who guided
your education across crowded streets to plays that transformed your
ten-year-old mind
how did you know how to find your way home¿

i do not wish to hurt anyone
i only wish for the wasps to stop hunting us
we wish to read and practice penmanship
                        to never have hunger for dinner
                                to love freely
Mr. Baldwin, i long for your guidance after you, too, have been buried

Black humanity in the face of police brutality.

FOR BLACK BOYS DRINKING ORANGE SODA AND SEARCHING FOR A NORTHERN STAR

i tell my Brother
"don't wear your hoodie,
keep your hands out your pockets,
be polite if an officer stops you"

i repeat the eldest black daughter parable
he rolls his eyes at the rehearsed speech as he slips out the door

i look at my Brother's smile all teeth and gumption
they will not see his jeopardy-winning grin
Emmett Till hat in hand, still in the august shade
Willie James Howard carrying his schoolbag with tenderhearted intent
Tamir Rice looking up at lego sets adorning his bookshelf
is all i see in my brother's empty bedroom

i tell my Brother
"don't wear your hoodie,
keep your hands out your pockets,
be polite if an officer stops you"

my baby Brother won't see the judge or jury coming, only the executioner
i repeat the eldest black daughter parable
i want to trip over his sneakers for the rest of our lives
that boy is growing like a magnolia tree, beautiful and tall for his age
they won't see the crooked way he wears his glasses
they won't see the cross he wears around his neck

he doesn't believe in god the way he used to,
but he loves my mother more than faith itself

i tell my Brother
"don't wear your hoodie,
keep your hands out your pockets,
be polite if an officer stops you"

they won't see him
and then i won't be able to trip over his sneakers anymore

my brother poured out a glass of grape soda to catch a moth
raced downstairs with the moth in his cup
a loose leaf paper with multiplication problems preventing his escape
he let the moth free outside our front door
i told him i would've killed it
he told me, the moth was trying to find his way home

i tell my Brother
"don't wear your hoodie,
keep your hands out your pockets,
be polite if an officer stops you"

my Brother is self sacrificing and clever and kind
i know my words cannot shield him
one day my words will not be enough to protect him
one day he will no longer be twelve
i will not be able to show him the way home

i tell my Brother
"don't wear your hoodie,

keep your hands out your pockets,
be polite if an officer stops you"

i repeat the eldest black daughter parable like a prayer depreciated prayer
thankful to trip over his sneakers

A dedication to Basquiat and the shared Black Latine experience.

CABECITA DE ELOTE

i don't feel like i should be holding your name
in my mouth
everyone talks about you
no one talks to you
you and i are of the same skin, bearing the same fruit
cabecita de elote, Jean-Michel—
how can anything be sweet after you ¿

we the uncanny
are not alone
only displaced
when i tell you i absconded from
their new york
i can feel you staring at me
eyes the size of saucers
egging me on for a response
i see you slouch into your armchair
and concede knowing
nothing has changed

in photographs Jean-Michel
the frame of your face familiar
i see you in little Black boys
proudly bringing their finger painting to their overworked mothers
i see you in the Queer kids skating through Park Slope
the Latinos packing an extra dulce de leche with a fatigued smile
full of ambition that their children have now inherited
i see you thirty years after your death

haunted by the strangers in the fetal position on park benches

at night when the police are just as feral

when you were fifteen

duérmete niñito, cabecita de elote, si no te duermes hoy, te comer coyote

A celebration of lifelong sibling antics.

MY KID BROTHER THE ASTROPHYSICIST

my kid Brother the astrophysicist with an attitude problem
time travels to the future

my Brother tells me i fucked up
and ceremoniously starts rummaging through my fridge
i contemplate calling my wife to argue about something that hasn't
happened yet
but if they tell me i've lost my mind
they'll be right this time

my kid Brother the astrophysicist with an attitude problem
drinks my orange juice out of the bottle
tells me i'm screwed as i swipe the bottle out of his hand

i ask him if this is his wretched sense of humor
if he got bitten by a radioactive spider
or if he's orchestrated an elaborate piece of mischief in May
(he's usually a little late)

my kid Brother the astrophysicist with an attitude problem
tells me in the future i have difficulty being his sister
i grew used to being his parent
now he's come back to be my friend
he tells me i lost all of my childlike wonder and whimsy
we drink orange juice out of the bottle,
paint on my living room wall,
watch X-Men Evolution

my kid Brother the astrophysicist with an attitude problem
completes our secret handshake

my wife isn't at all surprised to see him
they're always reminding me to smile
they slip him sugar cookies for the travel home

my wife carries me from the couch to the bed

Beyond the Binary: Lady Macbeth's Exploration of Gender in Shakespeare's *Macbeth*

By **Emilia Gillen**
Sponsored by **Sid Ray, Ph.D.**
English Language and Literature, New York

Lady Macbeth's role in William Shakespeare's *Macbeth* is unforgettable for many reasons, most notably for her exploration of gender. By challenging early modern gendered dualities through her ambition, meticulousness, and desire for power, Lady Macbeth makes a claim on what we would now call gender fluidity.[1] As an elite medieval Scottish woman, Lady Macbeth challenges traditional notions of femininity by breaking gender norms and boundaries, blurring roles deemed feminine and masculine, and embodying a three-dimensional character, even as she explores the darker side of the human condition.

Within the gender norms in medieval Scotland, Lady Macbeth holds the position of Queen, suggesting her desires for significant power, but the traditional subordinate position of women emphasizes the gender norms Lady Macbeth fights against but eventually transcends through gender fluidity. According to Laura Stoss, in her essay, "An Exploration of Conformity to Medieval Male and Female Roles in the Chronicle of Alfonso X," women in the medieval and early modern period were "confined into the roles of mother, widow, or virgin" (Stoss, 4). However, the positions for women in royalty were somewhat atypical:

> Royal women were given more opportunities than peasant women because they were responsible for the sustenance of the royal familial line. [...] Being politically active proved their capabilities to exceed the standard confines of the private sphere typically designated for medieval women. Nevertheless, royal women were still only deemed mothers, wives, and daughters and were excluded from the orders of society. Their importance was only to help males maintain power, and their influence in politics was normally temporary and sanctioned only by the fact that they were to help their son's or husband's rule (Stoss, 4).

---

1 The *Oxford English Dictionary* defines "gender fluid" as: "a. Not clearly or wholly male or female; androgynous; b. designating a person who does not identify with a single fixed gender; of or relating to a person having or expressing a fluid or unfixed gender identity."

As I will show, since Lady Macbeth views her feminine qualities as insufficient in her ascent to power, she rejects her femininity and becomes something outside the binary and proves her capability to exceed the standard for women by pushing toward elevated power. As experts on queenship Carole Levin and Robert Bucholz write: "the unusual combination of their gender and royal authority gave these women an opportunity to redefine power and gender roles (as applied to royal women, anyways) by exploiting the ambiguity involved in the status of being a female king" (xvii). As noted before, Lady Macbeth is an elite and royal woman, so the expectations set for her are different than those of a civilian woman. However, Lady Macbeth still escapes and challenges societal limitations throughout the play, and her pursuit of power involves a negotiation of traditional gender norms to achieve, through gender fluidity, something like the status of a "female king."

For Lady Macbeth, gender presents as unfixed; and the roles can be defied socially and psychologically. Her yearning for an identity beyond gender binaries, may be explained by recent queer theory. In her article, "Feminism without 'Gender Identity,'" Anca Gheaus uncovers the different layers of gender identity, one of which being an aspirational role:

> According to the fourth proposal, "gender identity" refers to the gender norms that a person wishes that others applied to them; it is one's aspirational gender role. To be cis, on this view, is to wish to occupy the gender role that corresponds to one's sexual characteristics. [...] Gender identity consists in identification with a social role, and maybe also with others who occupy that role (Gheaus, 42).

Gheaus argues that gender identity can function as the role people wish to be viewed as. Lady Macbeth's radical rejections of her designated gender role in exchange for a fluid role allows her to assume agency and power. Within this context, Gheaus' interpretation insinuates that Lady Macbeth's aspirational approach to gender through fluidity reveals her wish to escape the restrictions of her assigned gender that fulfills her thirst for higher authority, thus illuminating the flexibility of gender as not tied to sexual characteristics.

A close reading of Lady Macbeth's unsexing illustrates these points. When the audience first meets Lady Macbeth in Act 1, Scene 5, she exhibits interest in crossing the gender divide. Here, Lady Macbeth reads a letter written by Macbeth about his encounter with the witches, or the Weird Sisters:

> They met me in the day of success, and I have learned by
> the perfect'st report they have more in them than mortal

knowledge. When I burned in desire to question them further, they made themselves air, into which they vanished (1.5.1-5).

Lady Macbeth's reaction displays unbounded eagerness, which, to many, is evidence of her intense ambition to embrace the prophecy, but her almost instantaneous mirroring of the witches' identity in Act 1 suggests that her eagerness is connected to the gender ambiguity of the witches, inspiring her own gender exploration. Lady Macbeth's interest is piqued by the word "weird." The *Oxford English Dictionary* defines "weird" as: "Partaking of or suggestive of the supernatural; of a mysterious or unearthly character; unaccountably or uncomfortably strange; uncanny." Connecting the meanings of "weird" with the witches' gender ambiguity (or the choice to be "agender"[2]) suggests that the weird sisters are above natural beings with a genderless identity, who then encourage Lady Macbeth to contemplate her own gender identity as fluid. Contrasting the witches, as I will show, Lady Macbeth never fully withdraws from gender altogether, but instead formulates a combination of gender identities to establish herself as gender fluid.

Lady Macbeth asserts gender fluidity in her 'Unsex me" soliloquy. In Act 1, Scene 5 Lady Macbeth pleads with the supernatural forces to transform her: "Come, you spirits / That tend on mortal thoughts, unsex me here / And fill me from the crown to the toe topfull / Of direst cruelty" (1.5.39-42). Within this soliloquy, Lady Macbeth classifies gender as mutable and defies conventional femininity. As Lady Macbeth learns of the prophecy for Macbeth to become king, she visualizes her own potential to be queen. Although already elite, Lady Macbeth understands the limitations she holds being a woman, so she seeks transformation by asking to be "unsexed," willingly stripping her femininity and adopting a more fluid sexual alignment, leaving her unconstrained by her biological sex. The witches thus serve as a vehicle that drives Lady Macbeth to discover her gender fluidity as she aspires to be like these "uncanny" beings who are "uncomfortably strange." As gender identity can stem from an adoption of roles and predetermined sexual characteristics, Lady Macbeth follows the concept of gender as an aspirational role. Expressing a desire to be filled with "direst cruelty," she highlights her willingness to embrace malicious qualities, exceeding traditional notions for royal women as Lady Macbeth adheres to Ghaeus' perspective on gender identity which corresponds to a concept found internally within the self, aside from sex.

Within the staging for Act 1, Scene 5, the distinct nature of Elizabethan performances aids in deepening the fluidity of Lady Macbeth's gender. Shakespeare's Original Practices involved a gender masquerade, where

---

2 The *Oxford English Dictionary* defines "agender" as follows: "Designating a person who does not identify as belonging to a particular gender; of or relating to such people."

all female characters were performed by young male actors which creates a layered contradiction for Lady Macbeth's character arc. The young male actor playing her has embodied her original femininity, but then rejects it as Lady Macbeth asks to be "unsexed." The cycle of a male actor performing as a female character who does not want to be tied to femininity blurs the specific distinctions between her gender identity and intensifies her gender fluidity. This cycle within the performance subverts the ideas of gender being fixed and amplifies the idea of Elizabethan performances as fluid in nature while emphasizing gender as an illusion.

Two scenes later, a transformed Lady Macbeth mocks stereotypical expectations and "motherly" nature. In Act 1, Scene 7, Lady Macbeth, in conversation with Macbeth about Duncan's murder, makes an analogy to nursing a baby. She states: "I would, while it was smiling in my face, / Have plucked my nipple from his boneless gums / And dashed the brains out" (1.7.56-58). In this scene, Macbeth has gone back on his word, and Lady Macbeth says she would never do such a thing, as be foresworn, and she uses an analogy of a baby to express her own unwavering willingness to commit the crime. As she does this, Lady Macbeth questions Macbeth's masculinity – Lady Macbeth prods Macbeth more and more to stick to his word because for her, even if the promise was to murder a (hypothetical) baby, she *would* do it and stick to it. Audiences often do not pay attention to the subjunctive mood of her statement and read this moment as Lady Macbeth saying she *will* kill an infant, although she is speaking in the conditional. In her essay, "Fantasizing Infanticide: Lady Macbeth and the Murdering Mother in Early Modern England," Scholar Stephanie Chamberlain writes:

> Although she may well fantasize killing an infant, Lady Macbeth expressly rejects the masculine power which would allow her to wield a dagger [...] what she craves instead is an alternative gender identity, one which will allow her to slip free of the emotional as well as cultural constraint governing women (Chamberlain, 79-80).

Chamberlain highlights an "alternative gender identity" using the antimaternal positioning as a vessel for Lady Macbeth, as the hypothetical baby allows Lady Macbeth to display her desires to extend beyond gender and dismiss traditionality. This infanticide fantasy further stresses how her ruthlessness doesn't equate to a certain gender alignment, and she falls away from the emotional constraints of motherhood. Lady Macbeth's retraction from motherhood, or even parenthood entirely, correlates to her aspirations to embody gender fluidity as she crosses the gender divisions more as the play advances. Furthermore, even though she does not appear currently to have children, Lady Macbeth harkens to a time when she nursed a child, which makes her analogy even more manipulative.

This antimaternal stance suggests that Lady Macbeth has achieved her earlier demand to be "unsexed."

Through her newfound position of commanding authority, manipulation, and assertiveness, Lady Macbeth further embraces the "masculine" role in her relationship with Macbeth. Later in Act 1, Scene 7, Lady Macbeth again demonstrates dominance over Macbeth by questioning his masculinity when he starts to have doubts over murdering Duncan: "When you durst do it, then you were a man; / And to be more than what you were, you would / Be so much more the man" (1.7.49-51). As Lady Macbeth challenges Macbeth's masculinity, she highlights her virility in their relationship, as she is not inferior in their dynamic. The intensity Lady Macbeth holds over Macbeth while she continuously diminishes his manliness and accuses him of losing his manhood relays back to her fluctuation of gender statuses to emphasize her fluid identity. In her essay, "Masking Femininity: Women and Power in Shakespeare's *Macbeth*, *As You Like It*, and *Titus Andronicus*," Kelly Sorge, discussing the Shakespeare characters Lady Macbeth, Rosalind, and Tamora, writes: "These women are only powerful when they can control the men around them, and they lose that power when men feel threatened by the effects of female speech and sexuality" (Sorge, 2). Lady Macbeth's ascent to power goes beyond her manipulation and control of Macbeth and instead involves her interaction with gender. Lady Macbeth's ambition to break gender boundaries ultimately allows for her pursuit of power and her dictation of her position and status as a royal woman.

The plan to murder the king highlights the extent to which ambition drives her manipulation: "We fail? / But screw your courage to the sticking place / And we'll not fail" (1.7.59-61). Here, Lady Macbeth emphasizes her influence and dominion as she creates the plan and convinces him, and he agrees. Macbeth is insecure and precarious, while Lady Macbeth is unwavering in her plan – Lady Macbeth is not worried at all which allows her to convince him and that same potent ability to manipulate her husband reflects her extreme assertiveness in the relationship. Lady Macbeth makes Macbeth seem weak, and now his promise is less meaningful. Strangely, Macbeth is impressed. In the same scene, Macbeth states: "Bring forth men-children only; / For thy undaunted mettle should compose / Nothing but males" (1.7.72-74). Lady Macbeth's fierceness and security is so prevalent that Macbeth notes she would only bear male children because of the intrepidity and influential masculinity she possesses. In her essay, "Born of Woman: Fantasies of Maternal Power in MacBeth," Janet Adelman writes: "Lady Macbeth notoriously makes the murder of Duncan the test of Macbeth's virility; if he cannot perform the murder, he is in effect reduced to the helplessness of an infant subject to her rage" (Adelman, 42). Lady Macbeth's inclination to take charge and make decisions creates the illusion that Macbeth himself has no agency, meaning that, when fluid, Lady Macbeth's power is unmatched. Lady Macbeth's gender fluidity manifests as an immutable and all-powerful combination relegating to herself and her position an overload of power. However, the irony of this situation arises when Lady Macbeth allows herself to dive into fluidity, while Macbeth does not. Lady Macbeth prods at him for not stabilizing himself in the position of a man, yet she is able to fluctuate throughout and beyond the gender binary.

As the play progresses to Act 3, Scene 4, the audience witnesses how, although Lady Macbeth encapsulates gender fluidity and the combination of genders, Macbeth still conforms her to a specific gender role and places her back into the binary while simultaneously preventing himself from gender fluidity. This dynamic specifically manifests during the banquet when Macbeth says: "You make me strange / Even to the disposition that I owe / When now I think you can behold such sights / And keep the natural ruby of your cheeks / When mine is blanched with fear" (3.4.113-117). Macbeth telling Lady Macbeth she alienates him from his nature of being a man suggests that he believes her reaction is not appropriate for a woman or a wife. Lady Macbeth does not adhere to the conventionality of a wife and Macbeth criticizes her composed stance as if she should be the one more vividly affected by fear and guilt. Although Lady Macbeth retaliates prior to the end of the scene, specifically by diminishing his manliness when he cannot control his emotions after seeing the ghost of Banquo and demanding: "Are you a man?" (3.4.59), Macbeth still represents the patriarchal system that Lady Macbeth's gender fluidity fights against. Macbeth's refusal himself to be fluid results in scenarios like the banquet scene where Lady Macbeth cannot fully cross the gender divide. As Macbeth struggles with retaining a dominant composure, his lack of accepting a malleable persona creates instability. Nonetheless, the pushback Lady Macbeth executes exemplifies how she assumes her power within the marital dynamic. Lady Macbeth's position in the relationship leads her closer to full embodiment of authority when she displays gender fluidity. This means Lady Macbeth's authority is not solely present when men are weak and threatened, opposed to Sorge's previous suggestion; Lady Macbeth gains control over Macbeth in orchestrating the murders of the guards and King Duncan, and further through her control within their relationship, through gender fluidity.

While Macbeth represents the system of patriarchy for Lady Macbeth within their dynamic, the psychological aspects of gender identity for Lady Macbeth arise. In her essay "Motherhood for All—Women, Men, Trans*, Inter*, Nonbinary and Agender-Persons—Examined Using the Figure of the Continuum," Christel Baltes-Löhr touches on this topic in terms of the psyche in gender identity: "The psychological dimension of gender describes one's feelings about and self-awareness of gender, and thus oscillates between ascription and adoption of gender identities" (Baltes-Löhr, 98). Lady Macbeth's awareness of her flourishing gender identity grants her the opportunity to sway between multiple characteristics of separate gender identities, as Baltes-Löhr suggests. As gender becomes a psychological state rather than physical for Lady Macbeth, this shift between alignments allows for immense potential for herself against the system Macbeth and other men, such as the king, represent. Now, the label of just being a wife to Macbeth no longer corresponds to her acquired identity and status found within her gender fluidity.

Although Lady Macbeth aids in orchestrating the murders and does not see Banquo's ghost, she is not a cold-blooded killer. Rather she is a three-dimensional character who explores the darker side of the human condition. In Act 2, Scene 3, Lady Macbeth faints immediately after Macbeth confesses to the murder of the guards – the only witnesses to the murder of Duncan. As Macbeth suffers through dissociative guilt in this scene, audiences and readers wonder whether Lady Macbeth actually faints or pretends to. As planning murders and striving for untouchable power can corrupt a person, it is possible Lady Macbeth truly faints because of the burden she holds. However, it is also in Lady Macbeth's nature to strategize and quickly create a diversion that will protect both herself and Macbeth from suspicion. Lady Macbeth has a desire for power but refuses to murder, which leads the audience to believe Lady Macbeth faints as an action to conceal what may be a brewing regicide confession from Macbeth.

As if the fainting were foreshadowing, in Act 5, Scene 1, the audience witnesses Lady Macbeth's actual mental deterioration for the crimes she has planned:

> Out, damned spot! Out I say! One – two – why then 'tis time
> to do't. Hell is murky. Fie, my lord, fie! a soldier and afeard?
> What need we fear who knows it, when none can call our
> power to account? Yet who would have thought the old man
> to have so much blood in him? (5.1.35-40)

Lady Macbeth undergoes burdensome mental decay from the murder of King Duncan; guilt consumes and physically haunts her. The "spot" symbolizes the moral stain left on Lady Macbeth and her futile attempts at cleansing herself of guilt, and the realization of what she and Macbeth had done. Within this scene, imaginary blood she cannot remove is rapidly staining her hands, which contrasts to Act 1 where she asks for her blood to be made thick. Blood could be symbolic of Lady Macbeth's own biological femininity (as she menstruates[3]) that she can never fully get rid of it, no matter how much she strives to be fluid.

---

3 While analyzing Lady Macbeth's character in relation to gender identity, it's important to note that menstruation is not a necessary symbol of femininity. Within the historical context, we can conclude that due to Lady Macbeth's assumed age within the medieval period, menstruation is applicable to her identity, but that does not mean it constitutes femininity as a whole.

The mental deterioration Lady Macbeth faces links to her inevitable loss of sovereignty and, ultimately, self-destruction. At the end of the play, Macbeth learns of Lady Macbeth's suicide which is often read to be an abrupt and dismissive reaction: "She should have died hereafter: / There would have been a time for such a word" (5.5.17-18). When Lady Macbeth rejected gender constructs, she had control and superiority over Macbeth. It is commonplace to read Macbeth as uncaring here because he appears not to recognize Lady Macbeth's death, but it is also possible that he is painfully affected. Sorge further writes about Lady Macbeth's destruction: "This shows the true evolution of Lady Macbeth's character. [...] Once she started feeling guilty for her crimes, she lost control and killed herself, becoming irrelevant to the now powerful Macbeth" (Sorge, 13). The mental collapse and death of Lady Macbeth arrives when the guilt and immorality overcome her. Although Lady Macbeth undergoes this change, her death is not irrelevant by any means. Without Lady Macbeth, Macbeth himself spirals and eventually reaches his own death. Adelman states:

> Initially construed as all-powerful, the women virtually disappear at the end, Lady Macbeth becoming so diminished a character that we scarcely trouble to ask ourselves whether the report of her suicide is accurate or not, the witches literally gone from the stage and so diminished in psychic power that Macbeth never mentions them and blames his defeat only on the equivocation of their male masters, the fiends; even Lady Macduff exists only to disappear (Adelman, 49).

Lady Macbeth never regains the full dominance she initially held; and without her in his world, Macbeth is lost. Even one as ferocious, influential, and elite as Lady Macbeth can undergo the feelings of guilt and agony.

As Lady Macbeth explores gender dynamics in the play, she in turn experiences misinterpretation. Lady Macbeth is a cunning and complex character and is meant to be portrayed as such on stage, and this portrayal of a complex woman on stage could lead to the interpretation of her solely embodying a power-hungry woman. The added notion of Lady Macbeth capitalizing on gender fluidity along with the darker characters of *Macbeth* being women, such as the witches (who conform to ambiguous gender qualities as well), could allow for an influx of readings lacking nuance and gender awareness. Some audiences interpret her character as one-dimensional and narrow-minded when she is the opposite. Lady Macbeth breaks gender binaries and smears the lines between her feminine and masculine sides, creating a fluid identity while emphasizing a secure, will-powered character. In her essay, "Gender in Shakespeare's *Macbeth:* Performances and Performatives," Christa Reaves writes:

> As females with powers beyond the natural with unnatural intentions, they are meant to be fearsome beings, and as such, they are certainly outside of the idea of Jacobean femininity—they certainly are not silent and obedient, and depending on the production, their chastity is unknowable or completely questionable. Their performance of gender, then, is not one that connotes a socially desirable femininity (Reaves, 23).

Lady Macbeth is certainly beyond what is considered to be traditionally desirable in a woman. She is often mistaken for pure evil.

Analyzing Lady Macbeth through a more feminist-historicist and queer lens allows the audience to understand her complexities. Reaves further writes in her essay: "we can find the humanity in her by taking what we know of her (anxiety over gender, lust for power, and a crisis of conscience) and breaking down the reasons behind it. [...] Even if we have not personally felt her pain, we are aware of it, and it makes us feel for her rather than dismiss her" (Reaves, 18-19). We can sympathize with Lady Macbeth because of the unique aspects of her storyline throughout the play. While Lady Macbeth holds an abundance of complicity in malicious acts, understanding her perspective, intricacy, and evolution allows for an empathic and nuanced interpretation of Lady Macbeth, that steers away from misogynistic ideologies.

Lady Macbeth's embrace of masculinity and femininity suggests, then, that gender roles are not immutable and that they can be transformed or defied. Thus, Lady Macbeth's actions challenge societal expectations of conventional womanhood.

Leaning into readings that reframe the narrative of female characters can emphasize the importance of unconventional perspectives. Gender-attuned readings reveal Lady Macbeth's complexity as a three-dimensional character and aids in her challenging the binary of traditional gender stereotypes while blurring the boundaries of gender identity. Lady Macbeth in Shakespeare's *Macbeth* serves as an unforgettable exploration of gender, not just a case study of feminine villainy.

WORKS CITED

Adelman, Janet. "Born of Woman: Fantasies of Maternal Power in *Macbeth*." *William Shakespeare's Macbeth* (2010): 33-60.

"Agender, Adj." Oxford English Dictionary, Oxford UP, December 2023, https://doi.org/10.1093/OED/4590540055.

Baltes-Löhr, Christel. "Motherhood for All—Women, Men, Trans*, Inter*, Nonbinary and Agender-Persons—Examined Using the Figure of the Continuum*." *David Publisher*, David Publishing Company, 2021, www.davidpublisher.com/Public/uploads/Contribute/607e7b450ff6e.pdf.

Chamberlain, Stephanie. "Fantasizing Infanticide: Lady Macbeth and the Murdering Mother in Early Modern England." *College Literature*, vol. 32, no. 3, 2005, pp. 72–91. *JSTOR*, http://www.jstor.org/stable/25115288.

"Gender-fluid, Adj." Oxford English Dictionary, Oxford UP, September 2024, https://doi.org/10.1093/OED/9848587690.

Gheaus, Anca. "Feminism without 'Gender Identity.'" *Sage Journals*, Sage Publications, 2023, journals.sagepub.com/home/ppea.

Levin, Carole, and Robert O. Bucholz. *Queens & Power in Medieval and Early Modern England.* University of Nebraska Press, 2009.

Reaves, Christa. "Gender in Shakespeare's *Macbeth*: Performances and Performatives." *Louis University of Alabama Huntsville*, 2014, louis.uah.edu/cgi/viewcontent.cgi?article=1080&context=uah-theses.

Shakespeare, William, and Michel Garneau. *Macbeth*. Éditions Somme Toute, 2018.

Sorge, Kelly. "Masking Femininity: Women and Power in Shakespeare's *Macbeth*, *As You Like It*, and *Titus Andronicus*." *Scholars University of New Hampshire*, 2017, scholars.unh.edu/cgi/viewcontent.cgi?article=1327&context=honors.

Stoss, Laura R. "An Exploration of Conformity to Medieval Male and Female Roles in the Chronicle of Alfonso X." *The ScholarShip at ECU*, East Carolina University, 1 Jan. 2013, thescholarship.ecu.edu/items/f84ef457-a230-4ba8-bddb-72a5982d5af2.

"Weird, Adj., Sense 2.a." Oxford English Dictionary, Oxford UP, September 2024, https://doi.org/10.1093/OED/1146282251.

The Experience of Words: Gertrude Stein and Her Synesthetic Exploration of Language

By **Emily Whitehill**
Sponsored by **Erica Johnson, Ph.D.**
English Language and Literature, New York

How do we see words? Are they mere building blocks to convey a message, or do they transcend their literal meanings for a deeper experience? In the realm of synesthesia, a mode of cognitive perception that incorporates sensory information and how individuals interpret their senses, words take on a multifaceted nature that defies conventional perception. They become sounds and tones that create melodies and sympathies, merging the sensory experience. Words can serve as paint, bringing to life vivid images that blend language with the visual and emotional. With the written word, one pair of eyes may see text on the page, another a window to artistry and creation. Many authors and artists alike create sensory experiences for their audiences, dimensionalizing their works. One such author that did this was Gertrude Stein. Whereas many writers create visual images for their audiences, Gertrude Stein may be the first to write a form of synesthetic literature.

A renowned writer of the modernist movement, Stein's most successful book was her 1933 novel, *The Autobiography of Alice B. Toklas*, in which there was a quote that leapt from the page and resonated so deeply in me, so much so I could not ignore it. She described her experience of language as the following: "You see I feel with my eyes and it does not make any difference to me what language I hear, I don't hear a language, I hear tones of voice and rhythms, but with my eyes I see words and sentences and there is for me only one language and that is english" (Stein, 70). Gertrude Stein is infamous for her wacky and complex use of language in her poetry and writings, many people failing to make sense of it. However, this explanation provides an understanding of how she interprets the meaning of language in her brain. This experience aligns very well with the neurological function of synesthesia.

Synesthesia is not a disease, nor is it a medical condition. It is a phenomenon that occurs when people experience a blending of the senses. "Some people describe it as having 'wires crossed' in their brain because it activates two or more senses when there's only a reason for one sense to activate" (Cleveland Clinic, para. 1). For example, a person with grapheme-color synesthesia (one of the types I have) might see letters or numbers as colors, while someone with sound-color synesthesia might perceive sounds as specific colors. People with synesthesia are known for their creativity and many artists and creatives are known to have had it. With the way Gertrude Stein describes how she sees language, as well as her creative career as an author and art collector, it would be fair to assume she had synesthesia, and yet no critic has yet done so.

Gertrude Stein was an American author and art collector during the modernist period. Born in 1874 in Allegheny, Pennsylvania, she later moved to Paris, France where she would become a key figure amongst artists, authors, and intellectuals. Many would frequent her salon at her 27 rue de Fleurus apartment where she was renowned for her gatherings of many notable figures of the early 20th century. Attendees included: Pablo Picasso, Henri Matisse, Ernest Hemingway, Paul Cezanne, Eric Satie, Édouard Manet, and F. Scott Fitzgerald among many others. These parties helped create connections and collaborations, and her role as a supporter of these emerging artists and writers made her an essential part of the modernist movement. A great insight into these evenings comes from Gertrude Stein's *The Autobiography of Alice B. Toklas* where so much of the story takes place during these get- togethers. Despite the title, the book is not an autobiography written by Alice B. Toklas, Stein's life-long companion, but rather is Stein's own autobiography told from Toklas's perspective. This choice of narrative voice offers a deeply personal and nuanced account of Stein's life. The couple shared a long and deeply intimate relationship that lasted over 39 years. Toklas played a crucial role in Stein's literary career, they traveled together, lived together, and shared many of the same interests, including their love for art and literature. Stein and Toklas' relationship was marked by deep affection, loyalty, and mutual respect, which is seen in this intimate retelling of Toklas' life from the eyes of the person she loved the most.

Listening to Stein's experimental and avant-garde poetry when read aloud creates an additional sensory experience through the rhythm of her words. This synesthetic approach to language can evoke the sense of hearing movement in the language, much like in a piece of music. In her poem *If I Told Him, A Completed Portrait of Picasso,* though the words when read on a page may not make complete sense at first read-through, the melody of the sounds produced add a further layer to the piece. "Shutters shut and shutters and so shutters shut and shutters and so and so shutters and so shutters shut and so shutters shut and shutters and so. And so shutters shut and so and also. And also and so and so and also" (Stein, lines 15-17). From this quote, we hear her focus on sound, rhythm, and repetition rather than traditional narrative or descriptive elements and how this melody can evoke an emotional response for the listener. For some this may have a soothing, hypnotic effect, others may have feelings of confusion, frustration, or discomfort. She is playful in her manipulation of language and encourages engagement with the text in a more open-ended and interpretive way.

For those with grapheme-color synesthesia like myself, Stein's manipulation of language and focus on sound and rhythm creates a vibrant visual experience too. Each word or letter is associated with a specific color, transforming the text into a dynamic, colorful tapestry. I do not simply hear the melodic repetition; I see it in waves of color, each letter's hue blending and contrasting with the ones next to it creating a painting without the words. This visual component adds a layer of depth to the emotional response. I find that the colors shift in rhythm with the words, creating a multi-sensory experience that strengthens the emotional engagement with the text. Stein's use of playful language becomes not just an auditory experience but a visual and emotional journey for readers in this synesthetic literary form she has created.

Gertrude Stein's writing style is known for its repetition and rhythmic patterns. "In Gertrude Stein's writing, she utilizes this strategy of repetition to inject a deeper and more expansive significance to her words" (Sitrin, para. 4). Through repetition, she transforms language into a musical experience, inviting readers to engage with her work on multiple levels and discover new layers of meaning. Her famous phrase "A rose is a rose is a rose" (Stein, line 15) from her poem *Sacred Emily* is one of her most well-known lines. With each repetition, the word takes on a new meaning and changes the significance. This creates an abnormal experience for the reader, as it tricks the mind into believing the words hold more power than it first appears.

It is with Gertrude Stein's exploration of sound in both verbal and written language that I believe she has a form of synesthesia, as she seemed to perceive language not just as a means of conveying meaning, but also as an auditory and rhythmic experience. "Stein was engaged with sound as the basic nature within the voice as it occurs in both verbal and in written language as theory" (Mafe, 23). Stein's engagement with the fundamental nature of sound within the voice could imply a blending of senses as she approached language. This attention to the auditory dimensions of language demonstrates how Stein transcended traditional boundaries in her work, something that modernist authors are known for doing in this period of literature. This synesthetic approach to language allowed her to create a unique and immersive literary experience for her audience, something very revolutionary. In Stein's view, language was more than just a means of communication; it was a multisensory experience that intertwined sound, meaning, and form. "Synesthesia is illustrative for the importance of the extraction of meaning from stimuli for inducing phenomenal experiences. The interplay between the physical synesthesia-inducing stimulus and the way semantic associations finally shape the phenotype of synesthesia helps us to realize that semantics shape our experiences" (van Leeuwen et al., para. 31). Stein's unique synesthetic approach to language reflects the essence of this quote about synesthesia. Just as synesthesia shows the physical properties of stimuli, like sounds or written words, and their semantic associations to create a unique sensory experience, Stein's use of language seeks to evoke a similar multisensory response. Her repetitive and rhythmic writing style is designed to engage the reader's senses on multiple levels to evoke sensory and emotional experiences.

Gertrude Stein's agency of language is a testament to her deep respect for the English language and its expressive possibilities. In *The Autobiography of Alice B. Toklas,* where Stein writes about herself and her processes through the eyes of her partner, she explains how "She tried a bit inventing words, but she soon gave that up. The English language was her medium and with the English language the task was to be achieved, the problem solved. The use of fabricated words offended her, it was an escape into imitative emotionalism" (Stein, 119). Stein sought to achieve her artistic goals within language as a medium. Her approach was not about inventing new words, but rather about harnessing the potential of language, finding innovative ways to manipulate its structure and rhythm to capture her thoughts and experiences. What is interesting is it seems that Stein viewed the English language as the paints to craft larger works of art. Despite living in France and almost rejecting her Americanism (in a sense that both she and Alice very much considered Europe to be their home), English remained the language she would favor in her artistic approaches. Even German, the language she grew up speaking with her German immigrant parents, took a backseat to English. This shows how Stein saw flexibility within the English language to use it as her medium whilst also placing her in the larger context and community of modernist authors throughout the world.

In Gertrude Stein's *Tender Buttons*, her poetry collection published in 1914, her most individualized and uniquely composed poetry is showcased. This fragmented collection, categorized into three sections – Objects, Food, and Rooms – stands out in literary experimentation as the reader tries to find the meaning of the seemingly nonsensical sentences. "If lilies are lily white if they exhaust noise and distance and even dust, if they dusty will dirt a surface that has no extreme grace, if they do this and it is not necessary it is not at all necessary if they do this they need a catalogue" (Stein, 6). This is the pinnacle of Stein's works and her avant-garde style. I imagine Gertrude Stein crafting words and rhythms like she is working on a painting much like those she collected and displayed in her salon. Using words like Play-Doh as she creates a Frankenstein of literary madness. Whilst Stein broke down and reconstructed the conventions of the narrative, her fellow partygoer, Pablo Picasso did the same with visual forms. While Picasso's art is not directly tied to the neurological condition of synesthesia, the ways in which he would create his abstract art through form and color creates multi-sensory experiences that can challenge viewers' perceptions and induce synesthetic-like responses.

This similarity in reconstructing the traditional into artistic expression leads me to believe that this creativity was channeled through Stein and Toklas' salon, as creative minds challenged innovation and the normativity of expression.

When I read Stein as someone with synesthesia, I find it an interesting and fun sensory experience. The most prominent form of synesthesia I have is Grapheme-Color Synesthesia, where I associate specific colors with letters, numbers, words, or symbols. When Stein uses repetition in her works, for me it creates a tapestry of colors corresponding to the letters and words in Stein's text. For example, in *If I Told Him, A Completed Portrait of Picasso,* each repetition of "shutters," "shut," and "so" is associated with the color red, and therefore it creates a pattern and visual rhythm that complements the auditory rhythm of the words. For people with synesthesia, her use of repetition and rhythm is experienced more vividly in a multi-dimensional sense as it can be perceived not only through the auditory patterns but also visual ones. This experience can form a kind of visual music that combines the rhythm and sound of the words with other sensory experiences, making Stein's works a rich, multi-dimensional experience. I believe Stein was aware of how people could experience more from her works than others much like the way she herself was able to interpret language and therefore rather than making her work accessible to the masses, she unapologetically leans into her creative flare, appreciating the sensory experience of language.

Stein created a synesthetic literary form that made her work and influence on the literary landscape so profound during the modernist period. While *The Autobiography of Alice B. Toklas* may be Gertrude Stein's most accessible piece of writing, conforming most to the traditional composition of words, and in it we get the insight into how her brain functions and seeks that playfulness and enjoyment that comes with exploring the boundaries of language. Through a deep dive into many of her works, I believe wholeheartedly Gertrude Stein had synesthesia as what she saw in language, and was able to create as a result, provided her audience with a beautiful sensory exploration in the art of words. "Stein is simply a figure who transcends her work: she is the avant-garde, the ignorant American, the literary cubist, the unapologetic lesbian" (Higbee, 3). Her influences and innovations in both the art and literary worlds make her stand out as one of the pioneers of the modernist literary period. In this fascinating world she so delicately crafts, words can transcend their traditional roles and intersect with our senses, offering a glimpse into the extraordinary ways in which some people, like Gertrude Stein, experience the world.

WORKS CITED

Cleveland Clinic. "Synesthesia: What It Is, Causes, Symptoms, Types & Treatment." *Cleveland Clinic*, 3 May 2023, https://my.clevelandclinic.org/health/symptoms/24995-synesthesia.

Higbee, Erika. ""Dance a Clean Dream": Agency in Language in Gertrude Stein's Tender Buttons." *Humanities Honors Program University of California, Irvine*, 2019, https://escholarship.org/content/qt21t8c1p5/supp/Higbee-Dance-a-Clean-Dream-2019.pdf

Mafe, Majena. "Soundage: A Practice-Led Approach to Gertrude Stein, Sound and Generative Language." *Creative Industries Faculty Queensland University of Technology*, 2013, p. 267.

Sitrin, Carly. "Making Sense: Decoding Gertrude Stein." *Deerfield: Journal of the CAS Writing Program*, no. 6, 2013-2014. *Boston University Arts and Science Writing Program*, https://www.bu.edu/writingprogram/journal/past-issues/issue-6/sitrin/#:~:text=In%20her%20poetry%20in%20Tender,words%20she%20chooses%20to%20include

Stein, Gertrude. *The Autobiography of Alice B. Toklas*. Knopf Doubleday Publishing Group, 1990.

Stein, Gertrude. *If I Told Him, A Completed Portrait of Picasso*. Poem. 1923. *Poetry Foundation*, https://www.poetryfoundation.org/poems/55215/if-i-told-him-a-completed-portrait-of-picasso

Stein, Gertrude. *Sacred Emily*. Poem. 1913. *Oatridge*, https://www.oatridge.co.uk/poems/g/gertrude-stein-sacred-emily.php

Stein, Gertrude. *Tender Buttons: Objects, Food, Rooms*. Dover Publications, 1997.

van Leeuwen, Tessa M., et al. "The Merit of Synesthesia for Consciousness Research." *Frontiers in Psychology*, vol. 6:1850, 2015, doi: 10.3389/fpsyg.2015.01850.

NATURAL &
SOCIAL SCIENCES

Nanopore-based DNA Barcoding of Herbal Medicinal Products Reveals Plant Ingredients Not Declared on the Label

By **Danny Miller**
Sponsored by **Jeanmaire Molina, Ph.D.**
Biology, New York

ABSTRACT

Herbal medicinal products (HMPs) are an ever-evolving market worth an estimated $199 billion dollars. However, the US Food and Drug Administration (FDA) does not regulate these herbal medicines. There have been instances of fraudulent (i.e. substituted/adulterated) herbal products in the US market exposed by DNA barcoding, which uses short genetic markers to identify an organism, typically with Sanger sequencing. However, Sanger-based DNA sequencing can only be used when herbal products contain only a single plant ingredient, not herbal products with multiple/mixed ingredients. In this project, we used Nanopore DNA sequencing to authenticate a total of 8 non-FDA regulated herbal medicinal products (HMP, 3 single and 5 mixed). Of the 3 single-ingredient HMP, 3 were sequenced using Nanopore, and we detected other ingredients not on the label (i.e. adulterated). Though some of the declared plant ingredients (not all) were detected in five of the mixed-herb HMPs, all had some level of adulteration, including plant species known to be toxic. Our research underscores the significance of Nanopore-based DNA barcoding to authenticate HMPs, especially in settings lacking stringent government oversight of herbal supplements.

INTRODUCTION

Herbal medicinal products (HMPs) are an ever-growing market worth an estimated $199 billion dollars that is predicted to reach an estimated $417 billion by 2033 (Future Market Insight, 2023). In the US, HMPs are available at local grocery stores, supplement stores and pharmacies, as well as online, providing an alternative, more affordable and accessible means of treatment when compared to conventional allopathic medicine. However, given a lack of regulatory procedures by the US Food and Drug Administration (FDA), it's no wonder we see cases of substitution and contamination of HMPs when examined through DNA barcoding, a molecular technique that uses short genetic markers to identify an organism (Newmaster et al., 2015; Molina et al., 2018). Companies often aim to maximize profits from every part of their operations. This practice likely leads to substituting higher-value species with lower-value ones in ways that consumers typically don't notice. However, identifying the exact stage at which contamination occurs is challenging because the FDA does not oversee HMP production.

According to Michel et al. (2016) and Molina et al. (2018), 10-20% of herbal products do not contain the plant declared on the label, based on DNA barcoding. The typical workflow for plant DNA barcoding involves extraction of plant DNA, amplification of an appropriate plant marker, Sanger-based sequencing of the marker (usually outsourced given the prohibitive cost of Sanger sequencers), and comparative DNA sequence analysis against a plant database to authenticate the product (Molina et al., 2018).

DNA barcoding started as a method of species identification first explored by researchers at the University of Guelph, when they used the cytochrome c oxidase I gene (COI) as a "global bioidentification system for animals" with which they were able to identify specimens with 100% accuracy (Hebert et al. 2003). The same approach can be applied in plants. In this method a specific marker gene is chosen, sequenced, and compared to a sequence database to identify the organism, in the same way a supermarket barcode can identify a specific product when scanned. In plants the most common DNA barcodes used include the chloroplast genes *matK* and *rbcL,* as well as the nuclear Internal Transcribed Spacer 2 (ITS2) region. ITS2, a nuclear ribosomal DNA sequence in eukaryotic organisms, was demonstrated to be a practical DNA barcode for authentication of HMPs (Michel et al., 2016; Yao et al., 2010).

As technologies have progressed since the introduction of barcoding, we are now dealing with a dichotomous approach to the DNA barcoding process. Sanger-based DNA barcoding has been the tried-and-true method of generating DNA barcode sequences for almost four decades (Shokralla et al., 2014). While more accurate, Sanger-based DNA barcoding is not the most cost efficient. Sanger sequencing devices can cost upward of $50,000 per device. If the costs of devices are too costly, looking to outsource sequencing would cost roughly $4-6 per sample of purified PCR product, up to 1000 bp (Cermak et al. 2020). Depending on the experiment conducted, Sanger sequencing could be significantly more expensive. With advancements in genomic technologies, DNA sequencing has become cheaper and more accessible; including Oxford Nanopore Technologies' MinION expansion product, the Flongle costing $90 per instrument and processing up 2.6 Gb overnight, boasting both time and cost efficiencies for small experiments compared to its predecessors.

Unlike Sanger-based DNA barcoding, the most important advantage of using Nanopore-based DNA barcoding is its ability to sequence thousands of DNA templates in parallel (Wang et al., 2021), allowing for analysis of mixed species HMPs as well as allowing for the detection of contaminants in HMPs. Sanger-based DNA barcoding can only be used to authenticate single-ingredient HMPs. It is unable to resolve mixed signals from HMPs that have mixed herbs (Molina et al., 2018). Given the ease of use and relatively low cost of Nanopore sequencing, we aimed to leverage this next-generation sequencing technology to advocate for FDA regulations on HMPs. At the same time, we sought to demonstrate an effective, scalable method of authentication.

MATERIALS & METHODS

Eight (8) HMPs (3 single ingredient and 5 mixed, with multiple plant ingredients) were purchased from drugstores in New York City and from online retailers. Table 1 lists the various HMPs sampled. All HMPs sampled were pulverized plant material contained within gelatin capsules. HMP brand names and the names of retailers were withheld to avoid legal consequences. HMP DNA for the 8 samples was extracted using the Qiagen DNeasy Plant Mini Kit. The DNA was then PCR-amplified using ITS2 primers (ITS2-u3 and ITS2-u4) from Cheng et al. (2016), and if this pair did not work, the primers ITS2-S2F (Chen et al., 2010) and ITS4 (White et al., 1990) were used in different combinations with the Cheng et al. (2016) primers. PCR products were run on 1% agarose gel, and subsequently sequenced using Nanopore, following the protocol for ligation sequencing of amplicons with PCR barcoding (SQK-LSK110 with EXP-PBC001). For the 3 single-ingredient HMPs, they were also sent out to Eton Bio (Union, NJ) for Sanger sequencing.

Data from both Sanger and Nanopore were analyzed in Geneious Prime (Biomatters Ltd). For Sanger, ab1 sequence chromatograms for forward and reverse sequences were merged, assembled and blasted against Genbank ITS2 database to identify the plant ingredient. Raw sequence data from Nanopore sequencing were imported into Geneious and *de novo* assembled to form contigs, and their consensus sequences were sorted by length. Consensus sequences >150 bp were BLASTed against the Viridiplantae ITS2 database (Ankenbrand et al., 2015), with the top 3 hits from BLAST obtained. If 2/3 of the top hits belonged to the same plant genus, that genus was noted for that contig; those that did not match this criterion were discarded. Genus-level determination was sufficient for our purposes given uncertainties common in plant species circumscriptions (Schneyer et al., 2015).

Sample type (Fig. number)	Declared plant ingredients on label (with corresponding scientific name)	Confirmed plant ingredients as expected on the label	Adulterants detected
single (Fig 1)	hoodia (Hoodia gordonii)*	Hoodia	Piper, Echinacea, Astragalus, Glycyrrhiza, **Apocynum**
single (Fig 2)	ginseng (Panax ginseng)	Not detected	Astragalus, Hedysarum, Pteris
single (Fig 3)	Kava (Piper methysticum)*	Piper	**Convolvulus**, Thymus, Tribulus, Astragalus
mixed (Fig 4)	Irish seamoss Chondrus crispus, Burdock root powder (Arctium lappa), Fucus vesiculosus, Black pepper (Piper nigrum)	Arctium, Piper	Ipomoea, Oryza, Saccharum
mixed (Fig 5)	Blood sugar support (Lagerstroemia speciosa, guggul resin extract (Commiphora wightii), bitter melon extract (Momordica charntia), licorice root extract (Glycyrrhiza glabra), Cinnamomum cassia bark powder, Gymnema sylvestre, yarrow flowers (Achillea millefolium), cayenne pepper (Capsicum annuum), juniper berry extract (Juniperus), white mulberry (Morus alba) leaf extract	Glycyrrhiza, Gymnema, Capsicum, Achillea	Allium, Echinacea, Foeniculum, Lolium, Medicago, Mentha, Moringa, Pallenis, Senna, Stevia, Trifolium, Vitex

mixed (Fig 6)	Menopause support Dong quai (Angelica sinensis), lemon balm extract (Melissa officinalis), red clover (Trifolium pratense), chasteberry Vitex agnus-castus, soybean extract (Glycine max), black cohosh root (Actaea racemosa)	Angelica, Trifolium	Allium, Apocynum, Carex, Glycyrrhiza, Hoodia, Malva, Moringa, Morus, Piper, Polygonum, Solanum, Sophora, Stevia, Tetrastigma, Tribulus
mixed (Fig 7)	Curcuma longa, Allium sativum, Zingiber officnale, Black pepper extract (Piper nigrum)	Allium, Piper	Capsicum
mixed (Fig 8)	Echinacea purpurea, Peppermint leaf (Mentha × piperita), Lemongrass (Cymbopogon citratus), Cinnamon Bark (Cinnamomum cassia), Licorice Root (Glycyrrhiza glabra), Spearmint Leaf (Mentha spicata), Fennel Seed, (Foeniculum vulgare), Cardamom Pod (Elettaria cardamomum), Rose Hip (Rosa canina), Ginger Root (Zingiber officinale), Burdock Root (Arctium lappai), Mullein Leaf (Verbascum thapsus), Clove Bud (Syzygium aromaticum), Stevia Leaf (Stevia rebaudiana), Black Pepper (Piper nigrum), Black Elderberry Extract (Sambucus nigra)	Stevia, Mentha, Echinacea, Glycyrrhiza, Piper, Foeniculum	Amaranthus

Table 1. HMPs analyzed in this study including 3 single-ingredient HMP and 5 mixed-species HMP. Declared plant ingredients on the label are indicated. Plant ingredients (genus level) we have detected using Sanger and/or Nanopore sequencing are indicated for comparison. Proportions of detected plant ingredients from Nanopore sequencing for each HMP are depicted in Figures 1-8. Poisonous plant species detected as adulterants are in bold.*

RESULTS

Nanopore-based DNA barcoding authenticated 8 HMPs: 3 single-ingredient and 5 mixed HMPs. Two of the three single-ingredient HMPs were confirmed by Sanger (product 1: *Hoodia* and product 3: *Piper*). Figures 1-8 depict detected proportions of plant ingredient detected by Nanopore. No HMP contained solely the advertised product, and the product in Figure 2 contained none of the declared product.

Hoodia gordonii

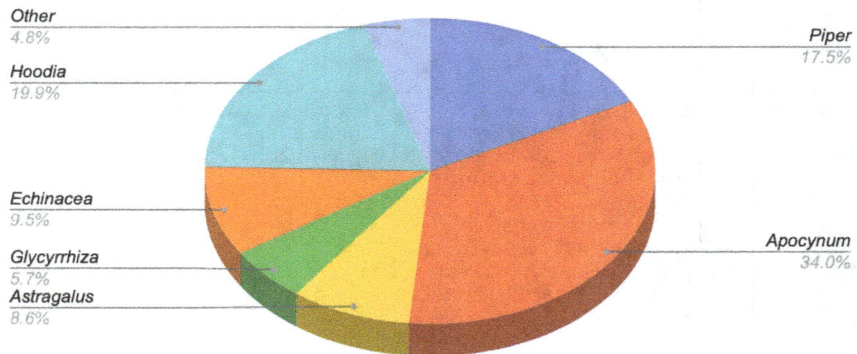

Figure 1. Proportion of sequence reads for all plants detected in single-species HMP labeled as containing Hoodia gordonii, *an HMP for weightloss.* Hoodia *was confirmed by Sanger sequencing, but Nanopore sequencing revealed other plant ingredients not on the label.*

Panax ginseng

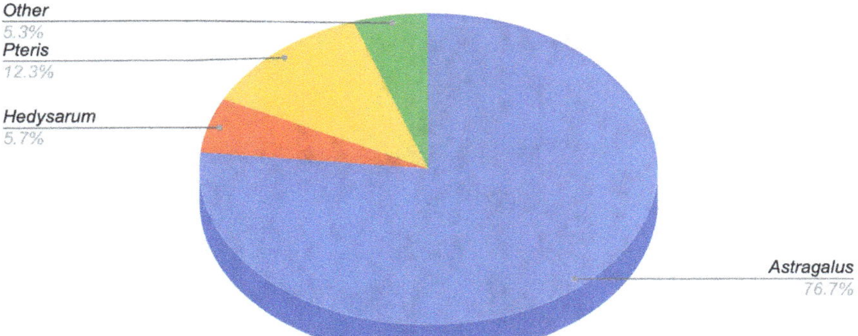

Figure 2. Proportion of sequence reads for all plants detected in single-species HMP labeled as containing Panax ginseng, *an HMP that works as an adaptogen (relieves stress). Sanger sequencing revealed potential substitution with* Astragalus, *which was also confirmed by Nanopore sequencing, along with other plant ingredients not on the label.*

Piper methysticum

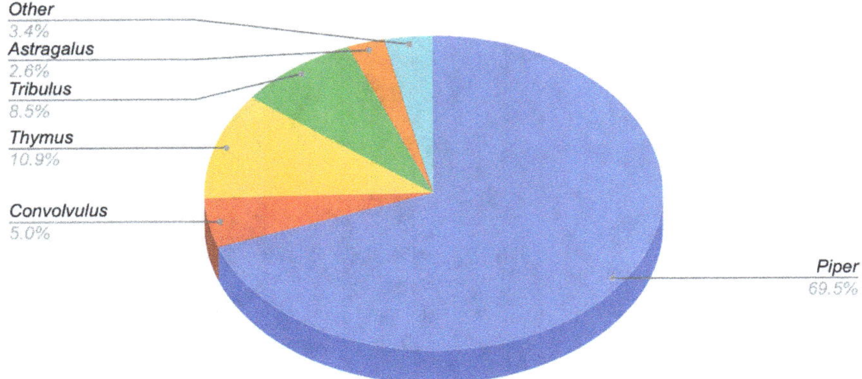

Figure 3. Proportion of sequence reads for all plants detected in single-species HMP labeled as containing Piper methysticum, *and HMP that reduces anxiety.* Piper *was confirmed by Sanger sequencing, but Nanopore sequencing detected* Piper *as well as other plant ingredients not on the label.*

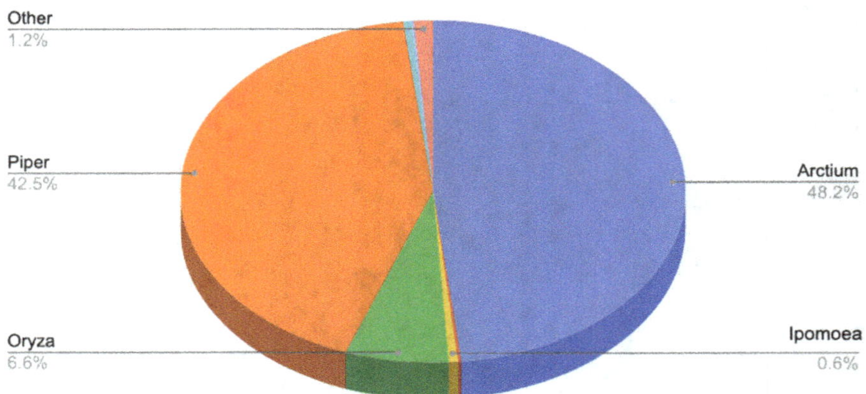

Figure 4. Proportion of sequence reads for all plants detected in mixed-species HMP, marketed to promote overall health. Nanopore sequencing confirmed presence of Arctium *and* Piper, *as declared on the label, but also detected other plant ingredients not on the label.*

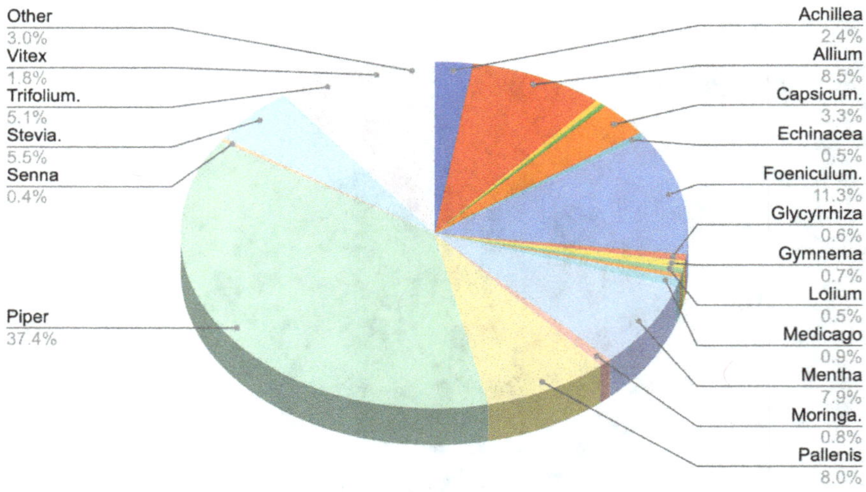

Figure 5. Proportion of sequence reads for all plants detected in mixed-species HMP, marketed for blood sugar support. Nanopore sequencing confirmed presence of Gymnema, Glycyrrhiza, Achillea, Capsicum *as declared on the label, but also detected other plant ingredients not on the label.*

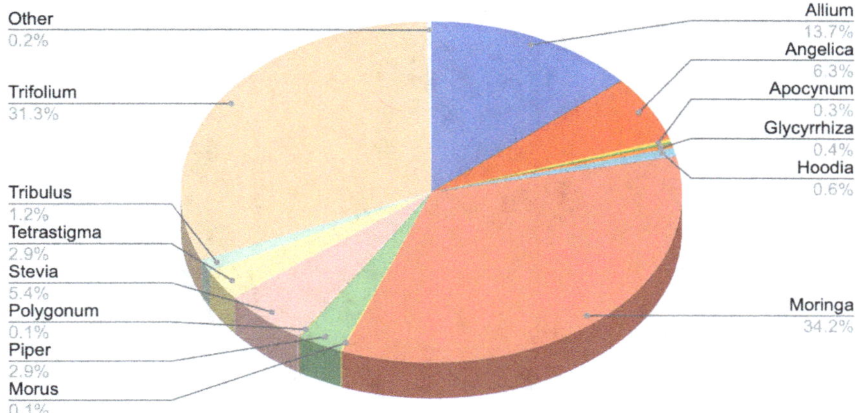

Figure 6. Proportion of sequence reads for all plants detected in mixed-species HMP, marketed for menopause support. Nanopore sequencing confirmed presence of Angelica *and* Trifolium *as declared on the label, but also detected other plant ingredients not on the label.*

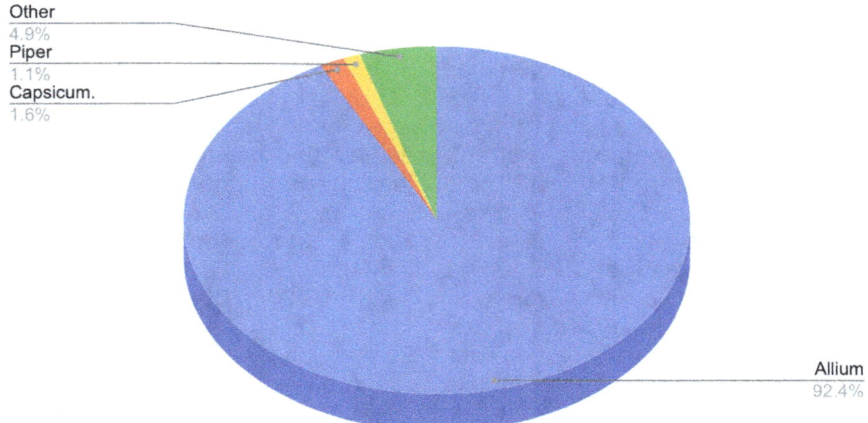

Figure 7. Proportion of sequence reads for all plants detected in mixed-species HMP, marketed for joint and immune support. Nanopore sequencing confirmed presence of Allium *and* Piper *as declared on the label, but also detected other plant ingredients not on the label.*

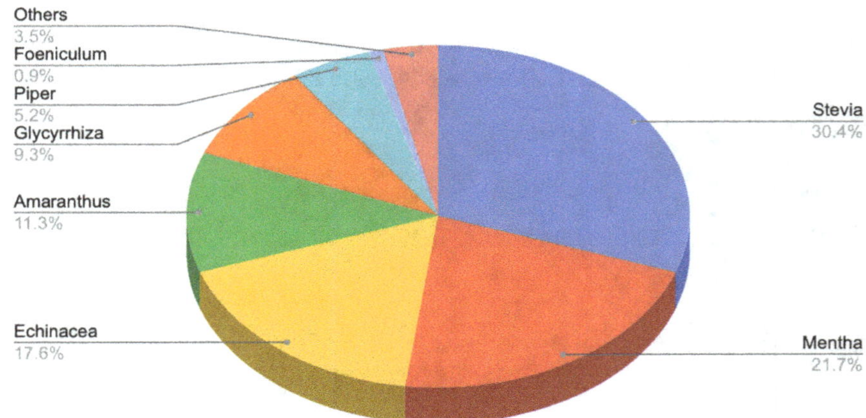

Figure 8. Proportion of sequence reads for all plants detected in mixed-species HMP, marketed for promotion of overall health. Nanopore sequencing confirmed presence of Stevia, Mentha, Echinacea, Glycyrrhiza, Piper, Foeniculum *as declared on the label, but also detected other plant ingredients not on the label.*

DISCUSSION

In this study we used Nanopore-based DNA barcoding to authenticate 8 HMPs: 3 single-ingredient and 5 mixed HMPs. Two of the three single-ingredient HMPs were confirmed by Sanger. Table 1 shows HMPs analyzed in this study with proportions of detected plant ingredients from Nanopore sequencing for each HMP depicted in Figures 1-8. Sanger sequencing was able to detect the declared ingredients but failed to detect contaminants for single HMPs shown in Figures 1 and 3. One contaminant that was undetected by Sanger in Figure 1 was *Apocynum,* a poisonous plant known to induce vomiting, coma, and death (USDA, 2018). HMP in Figure 2 shows a substitution, the product claiming to be *Panax*, but, instead, *Astragalus* was sequenced in both Sanger and Nanopore. This may have been motivated by the high cost of true *P. ginseng* reaching prices of over \$3,000 per pound (Arik et al., 2020) compared to *Astragalus membranaceus* at 1/100th of this price.

Of the 5 mixed-ingredient samples, some declared ingredients were identified using Nanopore sequencing. However, there were other declared ingredients that were not detected. For example, menopause support HMP, which supposedly contains 6 plant species according to the product label, only had 2 of these species detected (*Angelica, Trifolium*). On the contrary, there were undeclared plants that were sequenced and are contaminants (Table 1; Figures 4-8). Some may have been mixed inadvertently during manufacture of the HMP especially if the HMPs were processed in facilities that do not implement good manufacturing practices as defined by FDA. Unfortunately, some detected contaminants like *Apocynum* (Figures 1 and 6) and *Convolvulus* (Figure 3) are known to be toxic (NCSU, n.d. and Todd 1994, respectively).

Given the results shown here, no sample was purely the product advertised. HMPs either contained contaminants or had been substituted completely, which may be due to the lack of FDA oversight. From a consumer standpoint, these results are concerning, especially the detection of poisonous plants. Another concern is that these contaminants/ substitutions may trigger sensitivities/allergies in some consumers (Canadian Food Inspection Agency, 2018). The average consumer will not have access to barcoding technologies, so the consumption of these HMPs with unknown contaminants or substitutions could in fact be fatal if the wrong species is present in their product.

As demonstrated in this study, Sanger-based DNA barcoding can be useful for authenticating HMPs with a single plant ingredient, but it cannot detect contaminants in such cases. It is also ineffective for HMPs containing mixed plant ingredients. Nanopore-based DNA sequencing addresses these limitations by allowing for the identification of multiple ingredients and contaminants. This study highlights the issues stemming from the lack of regulation for herbal products, aiming to raise public awareness and emphasizes the need to improve the current regulatory framework, rather than undermining the value of these products. Given Nanopore's ease of use, which makes it feasible for undergraduate lab settings, and its cost-effectiveness, we recommend this technology for HMP authentication.

ACKNOWLEDGEMENTS

We thank Pace University's Biology department and Pace's Classroom-based Undergraduate Research Experiences (CURE) award to Jeanmaire Molina (faculty sponsor) for support.

WORKS CITED

Ankenbrand MJ, Keller A, Wolf M, Schultz J, Förster F (2015) ITS2 Database V: Twice as Much. Mol Biol Evol. 32(11):3030-2. doi: 10.1093/molbev/msv174

Arik, M., Gao, Y., Graves, B. (2020). Implications of changing supply chain dynamics of global ginseng trade: a pilot study. *Journal of Strategic Innovation and Sustainability*, *15*(1) https://doi.org/10.33423/jsis.v15i1.2729

Canadian Food Inspection Agency (2018). Undeclared allergens and gluten in herb andspice products–April 1, 2015 to March 31, 2016 and April 1, 2017 to March 31, 2018 https://inspection.canada.ca/sites/default/files/legacy/DAM/DAM-food-aliments/STAGING/text-texte/gluten_herb_apr_2015_mar_2018_1595527575667_eng.pdf

Cermak N, Datta MS, Conwill A. (2020) Rapid, inexpensive measurement of synthetic bacterial community composition by sanger sequencing of amplicon mixtures. *iScience*23(3):100915. doi: 10.1016/j.isci.2020.100915

Chen S, Yao H, Han J, Liu C, Song J, Shi L, Zhu Y, Ma X, Gao T, Pang X, Luo K, Li Y, Li X, Jia X, Lin Y, Leon C (2010). Validation of the ITS2 region as a novel DNA barcode for identifying medicinal plant species. *PLoS One* 5(1):e8613. doi: 10.1371/journal.pone.0008613

Cheng T, Xu C, Lei L, Li C, Zhang Y, Zhou S (2016). Barcoding the kingdom Plantae: new PCR primers for ITS regions of plants with improved universality and specificity. *Mol Ecol Resour.* 16(1):138-49. doi: 10.1111/1755-0998.12438

Future Market Insight (2023). Herbal Medicinal Products Market. https://www.futuremarketinsights.com/reports/herbal-medicinal-products-market [Retrieved 16 April 2024].

Hebert PD, Cywinska A, Ball SL, deWaard JR (2003). Biological identifications through DNA barcodes. *Proc Biol Sci.* 270(1512):313-21. doi: 10.1098/rspb.2002.2218

Michel CI, Meyer RS, Taveras Y, Molina J. 2016. The nuclear internal transcribed spacer (ITS2) as a practical plant DNA barcode for herbal medicines. *Journal of Applied Research on Medicinal and Aromatic Plants* 3:94-100.

Molina J, Sherpa C, Ng J, Sonam T, Stuhr N. (2018) DNA barcoding of online herbal supplements: crowd-sourcing pharmacovigilance in high school. *Open Life Sci.* 2018 13:48-55. doi: 10.1515/biol-2018-0007

NCSU, n.d. *Apocynum cannabinum.* https://plants.ces.ncsu.edu/plants/apocynum-cannabinum/ [Retrieved 16 April 2024]

Newmaster, S.G., Grguric, M., Shanmughanandhan, D. *et al.* (2013) DNA barcoding detects contamination and substitution in North American herbal products. *BMC Med* 11, 222. https://doi.org/10.1186/1741-7015-11-222

Shneyer, V.S., Kotseruba, V.V. (2015) Cryptic species in plants and their detection by genetic differentiation between populations. *Russ J Genet Appl Res* 5, 528-541. https://doi.org/10.1134/S2079059715050111

Shokralla S, Gibson JF, Nikbakht H, Janzen DH, Hallwachs W, Hajibabaei M (2014). Next-generation DNA barcoding: using next-generation sequencing to enhance and accelerate DNA barcode capture from single specimens. *Mol Ecol Resour.* 14(5):892-901. doi: 10.1111/1755-0998.12236

Todd, F (1994) Tropane alkaloids and toxicity of *Convolvulus arvensis*. *Phytochemistry* 39: 301–303, https://doi.org/10.1016/0031-9422(94)00969-z

USDA (2018). Hemp Dogbane *(Apocynum cannabinum).* https://www.ars.usda.gov/pacific-west-area/logan-ut/poisonous-plant-research/docs/hemp-dogbane-apocynum-cannabinum/ [Retrieved 16 April 2024]

Wang, Y., Zhao, Y., Bollas, A. *et al.* (2021) Nanopore sequencing technology, bioinformatics and applications. *Nat Biotechnol* 39, 1348–1365 https://doi.org/10.1038/s41587-021-01108-x

White T J, Bruns T, Lee S, Taylor J W (1990). Amplification and direct sequencing of fungal ribosomal RNA genes for phylogenetics. In: Innis M A, Gelfand D H, Sninsky J J, White T J, editors. PCR protocols: a guide to methods and applications. New York, N.Y: Academic Press, Inc. pp. 315–322.

Yao H, Song J, Liu C, Luo K, Han J, Li Y, Pang X, Xu H, Zhu Y, Xiao P, Chen S (2010). Use of ITS2 region as the universal DNA barcode for plants and animals. *PLoS One* 5(10):e13102. doi: 10.1371/journal.pone.0013102

Experiments with the Yeast *Saccharomyces Cerevisiae* can Shed Light on Important Biological Systems

By **Allie Van Pelt, Ellen Haverstick, Alessandra Barretta, and Josue Mendoza (Project 1); Anastasiia Kirdiianova, James Hill, Andrew Chen, and Isabella Birjandi (Project 2); Rebecca Korol, Yasmin Afaneh, Arnalyaliz Esparra, and Kc Kyara Carrasco (Project 3); Mark Shelan, Nicholas Samman, and Lucas Toledano (Project 4)**
Sponsored by **Daniel Strahs, Ph.D.**
Biology, New York

INTRODUCTION

The commonality and ubiquity of shared biochemical pathways between different organisms allows scientists to investigate pathways significant to human biological processes by using model organisms. One of these model organisms is the yeast *Saccharomyces cerevisiae*, commonly known as baker's yeast or brewer's yeast.

Biology students in the sophomore and junior year are asked to originate experiments using the *S. cerevisiae* as the experimental organism. This educational structure is a significant component of the inquiry-based learning paradigm in the Biology department. The students start by using the Saccharomyces Genome Database (SGD) (1) to investigate genes and processes of interest. Once these genes are chosen the students work on investigating the gene and developing their projects. This work is supported by the resources developed to support the yeast community, including the Yeast Knockout (KO) Collection (2;3;4). From this collection, students are able to obtain yeast knockout strains (e.g., that lack chosen gene of interest) supporting their experiments.

Following is a selection of the projects which were most highly evaluated by the Biology department faculty at our 2024 annual research day.

PROJECT 1: TESTING MULTIDRUG RESISTANCE MECHANISMS IN YEAST PDR1/8 MUTANTS EXPOSED TO A MUTAGENIC CHEMICAL

Saccharomyces cerevisiae possesses a complex drug resistance system primarily mediated by ATP binding cassette (ABC) transporters, such as PDR1, which maintain homeostasis via drug efflux (5). Essential for environmental adaptation, yeast utilizing intricate post-translational modifications regulate twenty-two ABC transporters. These transcription factors (TF) act as "sensors" for drug presence, triggering drug expulsion to protect the cell (6). While the long-term genetic aspects of pleiotropic drug resistance (PDR) are well-studied, underlying mechanisms must be considered to understand the initial transcriptional responses to drug resistance in budding yeast. The regulatory mechanisms governing PDR gene activation, *Figure 1,* forming the initial cellular signaling pathway with potential to confer long-term drug resistance, is a valuable field of yeast genetics research. Drug resistance studies in *S. cerevisiae* contribute to broader biological insights, as many molecular pathways are evolutionarily conserved across species, including human cancer drug resistance, where the PDR network resembles the human MDR network (7).

We investigated resistance mechanisms of PDR1 and PDR8 yeast KOs exposed to aminoglycoside antibiotic, which both encode C6 zinc finger TF's with a Zn2Cys6 binuclear zinc cluster DNA binding domain (10). Hygromycin B causes translational errors and disrupts ribosomal function (11). Hygromycin B is known to completely inhibit growth of wild-type (WT) *S. cerevisiae* exposed at 200µg/mL (11), preliminary experiments confer KO's had inhibited growth to the same concentration. Hydroxylamine mutagenesis induces a point mutation, specifically a cytosine (C) to guanine (G) mutation, which is a transversion, switching a pyrimidine to purine (12). This mutation could lead to genetic alterations affecting resistance to aminoglycosides, including hygromycin B. The exact mutation and effect of gene function can be identified via sequencing and BLAST analysis.

Hypothesis

If *PDR1/8* KO strains treated with hydroxylamine exhibit more growth in the presence of hygromycin B than untreated KO strains, then hydroxylamine-induced point mutations in *PDR1/8* KO strains improve resistance to hygromycin B. These mutations upregulate existing or activate new compensatory pathways in *PDR1/8*'s absence.

Hydroxylamine is utilized specifically because it induces point mutations, which allows for a more controlled and predictable mutagenesis to the KO strain's sequences than random mutagenesis.

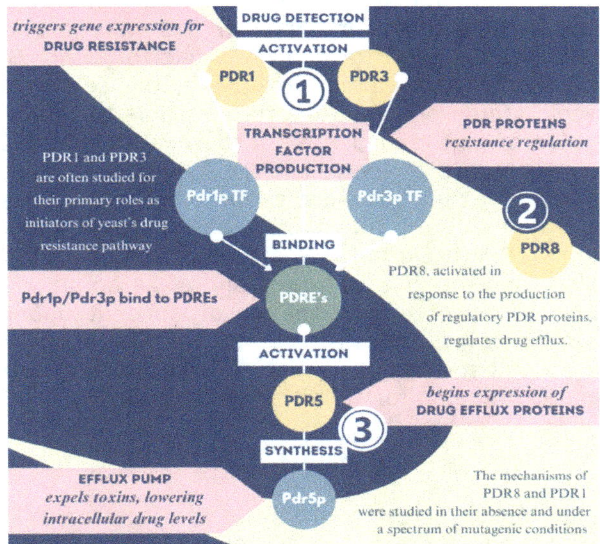

Figure 1: [Step 1] Within minutes of detecting a drug, yeast activates a cascade of PDR genes dependent on the protein encoded by PDR1, the Pdr1p TF. (8). PDR1, which is the key regulator of resistance genes in response to drugs or toxins, activates genes and increases expression of proteins which pump out or neutralize toxins, thus conferring resistance. [Step 2] Pdr1p and Pdr3p regulate PDR by binding to PDR responsive elements (PDREs), with their activity influenced by the flanking sequences of these sites and enhanced by binding to adjacent half sites (6). [Step 3] Pdr1p and other transcription regulators regulate PDR5, which is a gene encoding a membrane protein involved in drug extrusion which is also a member of the ABC transporter superfamily (9).

Experiment and Methods

Initial attempts to isolate a pure hydroxylamine crystal involved the use of a separatory funnel for the isolation and crystallization. For the experiment, a hydroxylamine hydrochloride and bromoethane (organic solvent) solution was reacted with a basic solution of NaOH to neutralize the HCl. Limited reagents and temperature control reduced yield, which became a determining factor affecting the isolation protocol. Thus, preparation of a free hydroxylamine solution rather than a crystal allowed for immediate dilution, pH correction, and treatment. We developed an experimental protocol using freshly synthesized hydroxylamine at three final concentrations: 5 mM, 10 mM or 20 mM hydroxylamine. Immediate use upon formation of each hydroxylamine solution at their respective concentration separately for each duration group offered consistent exposure conditions while minimizing risk with this mutagenic compound. Each yeast strain was exposed to hydroxylamine for either 30 minutes or 120 minutes. After hydroxylamine exposure, the cells were washed thrice with ice-cold sterile phosphate-buffered saline to remove residual hydroxylamine before being resuspended in Yeast Peptone Dextrose (YPD), media that provides nutrients for yeast, for a five-day recovery period. After five-day recovery, the cells were exposed to final concentration of 200µg/mL hygromycin B during incubation at 30°C and shaking at 200 rounds per minute (RPM). During this incubation, a spectrophotometer was used hourly during the first 10 hours, and at 24 hours and 48 hours to measure the cell density using the absorbance at 600nm. During the exposure and recovery phases, careful preparation of media and samples led to no statistically significant differences in initial yeast cell concentration measurements for each treatment group.

Results

Preliminary Experiment: To test hygromycin B effects on WT vs *PDR/8* KO strains, we exposed them to 200µg/mL hygromycin B. KO strains exhibited growth inhibition, confirming *PDR1/8* absence limits hygromycin B resistance, making this model appropriate for testing compensatory resistance mechanisms.

Experiment: To determine whether hydroxylamine-induced mutations can increase growth in KO strains when exposed to hygromycin B, we treated KO strains with hydroxylamine at varying concentrations and durations, then exposed to hygromycin B. KO strains treated with hydroxylamine showed increased growth in hygromycin B, indicating tolerance. Hydroxylamine appears to induce mutations which support growth under antibiotic stress, suggesting the activation or upregulation of compensatory pathways in these mutant KO strains. The strains treated with 20mM hydroxylamine for 120 minutes exhibited the highest growth in hygromycin B, with a significant OD increase compared to the unmutated KO control strains. These results indicate higher hydroxylamine concentrations and longer exposure times improve the KO strain's ability to tolerate hygromycin B.

In future experiments, the next step would be identification of the specific genetic changes that are responsible for increased resistance in mutant KO strains. Genomic sequencing and BLAST analysis can be conducted on relevant strains to identify recurring mutations or target regions linked with KO growth in the presence of hygromycin B.

Two *PDR8* KO strains (KO 6 and 4) when exposed to 120 minutes of hydroxylamine-mutagenesis, exhibit efficient drug resistance mechanisms. Under non-selective conditions, we observed lower OD measurements in both *PDR1/8* KO mutant strains compared to control strains under normal growth conditions, opposite to the effect of mutagenesis on WT strains. This decrease in growth can likely be attributed to the metabolic stress associated with activating alternative resistance pathways, which, without antibiotic stress, diverts resources from essential cellular processes.

PDR8 KO 24	**PDR8 KO 6**	**PDR8 KO 4**
Media: NON-SELECTIVE Mutagenesis: 20mM for 30 min This mutant strain exhibited a significant growth rate decrease. 	Media: CONTAINS hygromycin B Mutagenesis: 20mM for 120 min This mutant strain exhibited the highest significant growth rate increase. 	Media: Contains hygromycin B Mutagenesis: 5mM for 120 min This mutant strain exhibited a significant growth rate increase.
PDR8 KO Mutant — 1.699 PDR8 KO Non-Mutant — 2.17 Non-mutant control: highest final OD measurement of the entire experiment	PDR8 KO Mutant — 1.601 PDR8 KO Non-Mutant — 0.578 Enhanced growth under antibiotic stress. Our first indicator for further research into prolonged exposure.	PDR8 KO Mutant — 1.125 PDR8 KO Non-Mutant — 0.578 Enhanced growth under antibiotic stress. Hypothesis: prolonged exposure induces gain-of-function mutation for PDR8 KO strains.

Table 1: Summary of experimental conditions and results for various isolates of mutagenized PDR8 KO strains.

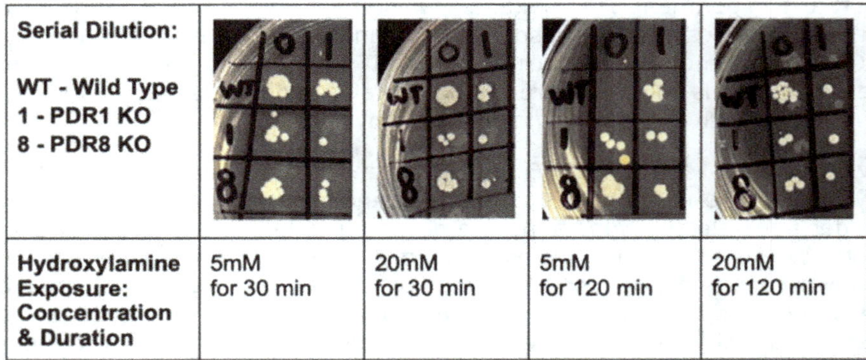

Serial Dilution: WT - Wild Type 1 - PDR1 KO 8 - PDR8 KO				
Hydroxylamine Exposure: Concentration & Duration	5mM for 30 min	20mM for 30 min	5mM for 120 min	20mM for 120 min

Figure 2: Spot assays of yeast at selected exposures to hydroxylamine on non-selective media. It is evident hydroxylamine exposure at higher concentrations and durations under normal growth conditions negatively impacts the growth of PDR1/8 KO strains.

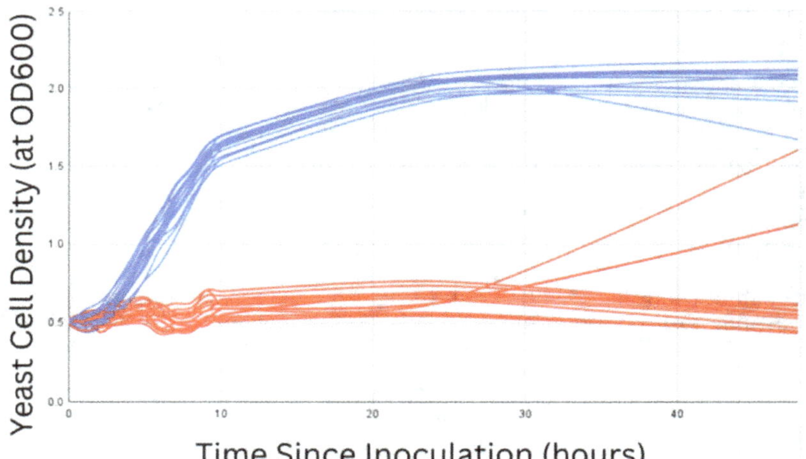

Figure 3: Blue: All mutant and control PDR1 KO, PDR8 KO, and WT groups under normal growth conditions (non-selective). Red: All mutant and control PDR1 KO, PDR8 KO, and WT groups under hygromycin B exposure (selective). Optical density (OD) values were compared to evaluate growth differences across strains and treatments. Growth curves for selective vs. non-selective conditions revealed three outliers; PDR8 KO 24, 6, and 4.

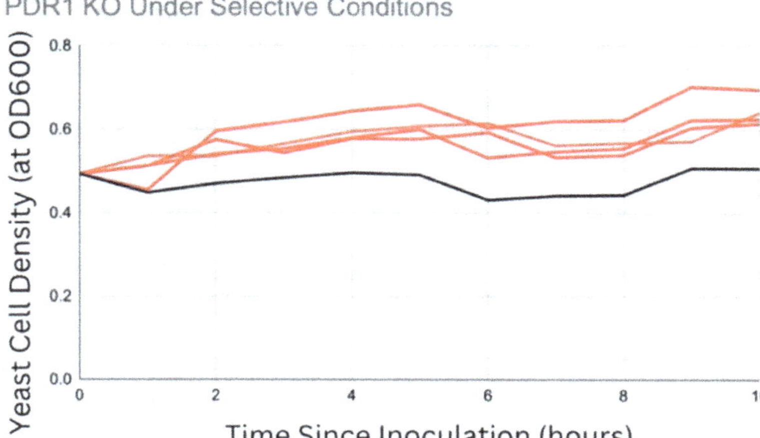

Figure 4: Red: PDR1 KO groups exposed to hydroxylamine mutagenesis. Black: PDR1 KO control group, not exposed to hydroxylamine mutagenesis Effects of Hygromycin B. Exposure on PDR1 KO Gene Variant Growth After Mutagenesis. The measurements were taken with a spectrophotometer at OD600. PDR1 KO strains (red) grown in selective media exhibited the largest statistically significant difference in mutant growth compared to control (black). Multiple KO strains were observed under various mutagenic conditions, their growth illustrated by the numerous red traces, all averaging more growth than the control strain.

Treatment for 120 minutes (about 2 hours)	P-value: 0.0024
Treatment for 30 minutes	P-value: 0.0016

Table 2: Repeated measures ANOVA was used to evaluate growth changes over time, comparing growth between each group treatment conditions. Significant differences were observed in PDR1 KO mutant growth post-mutagenesis under selective conditions through Mann-Whitney U and Wilcoxon Rank Sum tests. These statistical findings support the presence of hydroxylamine-induced mutations that significantly increase growth in media containing hygromycin B.

PROJECT 2: SPILLING THE TEA ABOUT FUS1 AND ARV1: GROWTH OF KNOCKOUTS UNDER AN ORGANIC ALKALIZING AGENT

The FUS1 gene is a facultative gene found in many eukaryotes. In yeast, particularly *Saccharomyces cerevisiae*, the *FUS1* gene encodes for the Fus1 protein, which is an integral part in the fusion of cell walls during sexual reproduction in yeast. Haploid yeast cells have two genders: "a" type and "alpha" type, which serve as "sexes" for the yeast. Once attracted to each other via pheromone release, "shmoo" tips extend from the cells to create cytoskeletal membrane projections that follow a pheromone gradient towards each other until cell fusion occurs. These projections serve as the site where the fusion pores will be created; membrane fusion proteins (like Fus1p) will be localized in that area (13).

Fus1p, encoded by *FUS1,* serves to help remodel the cell wall and plasma membrane so the single diploid offspring can be formed from the two haploid parent cells (14). The effects of a *FUS1* knockout gene can be seen during mating of two haploid cells. Overall, mating efficiency will be decreased, as cellular fusion of the two haploid cells will be partially impaired due to missing Fus1p in the cell membrane 15; 16).

ARV1 gene encodes for Arv1p which is an ER transmembrane protein that acts as a flippase in GPI anchor synthesis/biosynthesis that is essential for yeast growth (17; 18). Furthermore, Arv1p also plays a role in regulating sterol and sphingolipid homeostasis as well as levels of cholesterol and bile acid (19; 20). *ARV1* is also thought to be essential for mating and induction of the unfolded protein response in yeast (21; 22).

The *ARV1* gene is conserved across several fungal and metazoan species, including humans and it possesses clinical importance as several diseases including dilated cardiomyopathy, epileptic encephalopathy and other developmental conditions are *ARV1*-associated (23; 24).

Triethanolamine (TEA) is an organic alkaline ammonia derivative with ethanol groups substituted in the place of hydrogens. Its industrial uses include acting as surfactants and pH balancers in cosmetics. Biologically, it has been used to induce spermiogenesis in *C. elegans* and has been proven to serve as a nitrogen source in some fungal strains (25). For our purposes, TEA was chosen because it disturbs the membrane composition due to its ability to change pH and, therefore, can act as a stress factor under which FUS1 and ARV1 knockouts can be tested for growth and viability. To be more specific, changes in the pH affect both protein and lipid composition of the membrane and interfere with normal protein folding (26). Additionally, TEA being an organic base can directly interact with internal phospholipid structure, as opposed to inorganic bases. To reiterate, the focus is on the membrane because both of our proteins of interest are located in the phospholipid membranes (Fus1 in the plasma membrane and Arv1 in the ER membrane). Overall, the absence of these genes under treatment conditions may yield phenotypes that will uncover novel functions of both Arv1 and Fus1 proteins and TEA.

For our experiment, both *ARV1* KO and *FUS1* KO yeast strains were treated with triethanolamine (TEA) and we hypothesized that the growth rate of these strains would decrease as membrane composition is disturbed by the chemical.

Experiment and Methods

Six (6) YPD plates and 6 nutrient dropout plates were created. The nutrient dropout plates were created to be 2.78 mM dextrose, 101.9 mM postassium acetate, 0.5 g of yeast extract, and 7.5 g agar.

The reasoning for creating nutrient dropout plates, as opposed to using normal YPD for the FUS1 Wild Types and KO's, is because FUS1 is a facultative gene, meaning its expression only occurs under a specific condition and is not directly essential to the cells' survival. Since FUS1 is expressed only during mating of haploid cells, conditions must be created to induce the haploid phase, such as reduced nutrient availability in the media used. This will cause yeast cells to go into meiosis, producing haploid cells as a survival adaptation. Once in haploid phase, the FUS1 Wild Type and KO phenotypes can be observed and tested (27).

ARV1 "knockout" (KO), *FUS1* KO and Wild Type were inoculated in liquid YPD in conical tubes and grown in the shaking incubator for 24 hours at 31°C. Triethanolamine (TEA) was then added to create three solutions of *ARV1* KO, *FUS1* KO, WT and one solution of a negative control prepared with no TEA and 1 mL of yeast colony. TEA was tested with each strain at 1% and 2% concentrations. A second negative control was prepared by mixing uninoculated YPD with 2% TEA. Following TEA addition, tubes were then grown aerobically at 31°C for 24 hours.

Spot assays of the prior days inoculated cultures were prepared on the YPD and nutrient dropout plates. Spot assays were grown at room temperature: *FUS1* KO plates were checked after 73 hours while *ARV1* KO plates were checked after 5 days. Light microscopy was used with Trypan Blue staining to determine if nutrient deficient media was successful in inducing haploid phase in the *FUS1* KO strain. Experiments conducted with *FUS1* KO were performed with a haploid strain. In total, three trials were conducted, and the haploid phase was confirmed before each trial for experiments 1 and 3 to avoid any experimental bias.

Results

In order to test the effects of TEA on the growth of both FUS1 and ARV1, WT and KO phenotypes, all 4 strains were incubated in 0%, 1%, and 2% TEA solutions on their respective media types. As shown in Figure 4 and 5, FUS1 WT and KO both showed decreased growth with respect to increasing TEA concentrations, as expected. However, the treatment of ARV1 WT and KO strains yielded surprising results, as both spot assay and spectrophotometric analysis demonstrated an increase in growth of ARV1 KO as TEA concentrations increased.

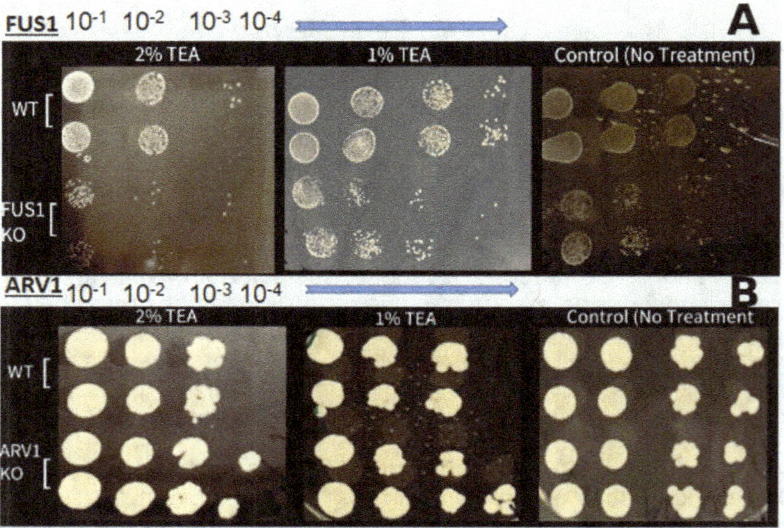

Figure 5: Spot assays were performed to analyze KO vs WT strains. FUS1 KO vs WT (A); ARV1 KO vs WT (B). The dilution factor and TEA exposure is indicated above each figure. FUS1 KO demonstrated decreased growth in all trials when compared to the WT strain and both WT and FUS1 KO showed decreased growth as the concentration of TEA increased. ARV1 KO has shown interesting results. Across multiple spot assay trials, ARV1 KO grew better under higher TEA concentrations, as can be seen in Figure 5B.

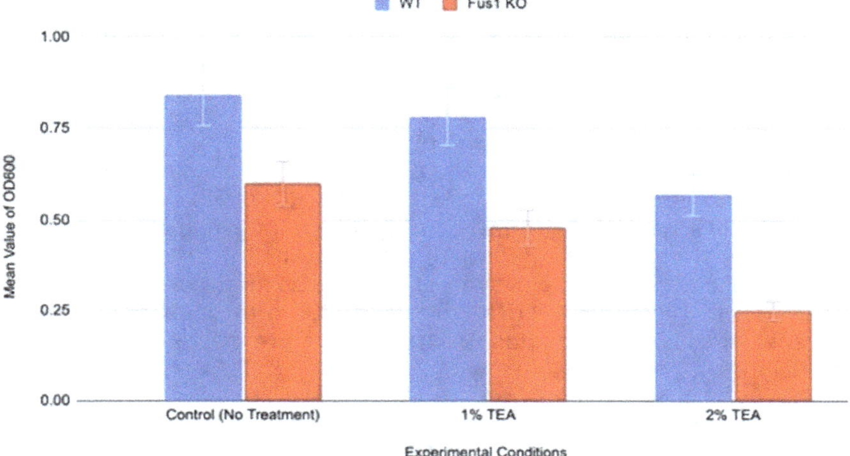

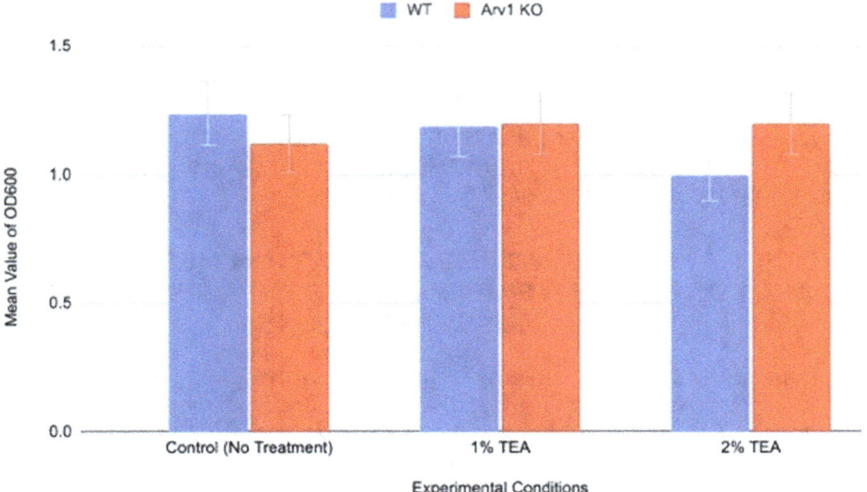

Figure 6: Growth curves of FUS1 *KO vs WT in nutrient dropout media (top) and* ARV1 *KO vs WT in YPD media (bottom). TEA exposure is indicated below each column.*

The yeast strains were also analyzed via growth in liquid media with exposure to TEA. The cell concentration was determined in triplicate using a spectrophotometer to analyze the mean growth values of WT and KO strains. *FUS1* KO and WT showed results that correlate with the spot assay. The growth curve of the *ARV1* KO did not show conclusive results as the mean growth was not statistically different from WT yeast.

Since we know that TEA affects the pH and, consequently, the membrane lipids' structure, we assume that the membrane becomes more fluid (28). As the membrane becomes more fluid, *ARV1* KO strain yeast cells have unregulated GPI-anchor synthesis during which intermediate compounds can flip by themselves across the membrane. Furthermore, sterol distribution and sphingolipid synthesis are also unregulated. Together, these factors might have led to the excessive growth of mutant *ARV1* KO yeast strains, but additional experiments are needed to draw any conclusions.

The *FUS1* KO strain, as predicted, grew less than the WT because *FUS1* is required for fusion pore control and shmoo tip growth. In addition, as the chemical fluidized the membrane, possible mating processes cannot be conducted properly leading to less growth. Some of the future experiments to conduct include the usage of high-powered fluorescent microscopy and membrane staining to study the ER and plasma membranes to observe conformational or structural changes in *FUS1* KOs. Additionally, gene expression may be altered by the TEA exposure and qPCR could be used to analyze the gene regulation in presence of TEA and our KO strains. Lastly, cloning of either the *FUS1* or *ARV1* genes can be conducted to rescue the phenotype and confirm that the growth differences are indeed due to the absence of *ARV1* or *FUS1* genes.

PROJECT 3: ASSESSING THE ADAPTATION MECHANISMS IN ARC1 AND BMH1 YEAST MUTANTS EXPOSED TO HIGH SALT CONCENTRATIONS

The yeast proteins *Arc1* and *Bmh1* play pivotal roles in various cellular processes, essential for the survival and proper functioning of the organism. *Arc1* is primarily responsible for the delivery of tRNA in yeast cells by binding tRNA, which stimulates catalysis and ensures proper localization (29). It binds both tRNA and methionyl-and glutamyl-tRNA synthetase, playing a crucial role in the regulation of organismal metabolism (30). This regulation is vital for coordinating cellular growth and metabolism in response to nutrient availability and stress signals. *Arc1* is also indispensable for the coordination of protein synthesis and autophagy, allowing yeast cells to adapt to fluctuating environmental conditions, which is critical for their survival and growth (31). Null mutant strains of *Arc1* exhibit reduced competitive fitness and heightened sensitivity to various substances, such as Congo Red, mycophenolic acid, paromomycin, acetaldehyde, and chitosan, as well as increased sensitivity to cold temperatures, which inhibit its activation.

Bmh1, also known as yeast 14-3-3 protein Bmh1, is integral to various cellular functions including signal transduction, cell cycle regulation, and stress response (32). It regulates multiple signaling pathways and processes such as DNA damage and spindle position checkpoints, filamentous growth, cell wall chitin biosynthesis, and aggresomal assembly (31). When *Bmh1* is expressed, the organism exhibits sensitivity to hyperosmotic stress while showing resistance to oxidative stress. Interestingly, overexpression of *Bmh1* results in slow growth, and previous research indicates that osmotic stress can cause rapid delocalization of the protein (33).

Understanding the roles and regulation of *Arc1* and *Bmh1* provides significant insights into the complex network of protein interactions and stress responses in yeast, highlighting their importance in maintaining cellular homeostasis and adaptability. Mutations in *Bmh1* may heighten cell sensitivity to NaCl-induced osmotic stress, thereby amplifying the stress response. Conversely, mutations in *Arc1* may not influence cell sensitivity to NaCl-induced osmotic stress, indicating no significant alteration in response.

Experiment and Methods

Bmh1 and *Arc1* yeast knockouts (KO) were obtained from the Yeast Knockout Collection. Prior to use, all strains were PCR verified for the presence of the knockout mutation. They were then exposed to different NaCl concentrations, and their growth and stress responses were observed. Wild-type and mutant yeast strains were spread on YPD plates and incubated for 2 days at 30°C. Single colonies were transferred into tubes containing YPD. Using a spectrophotometer at 600 nm, the growth curve of each culture was measured to determine the volume needed to reach an absorbance of 1.557. Each strain was diluted with 0.0068 mL YPD and 0.0932 mL yeast for Arc1, and 0.0052 mL YPD and 0.0948 mL yeast for Bmh1, to achieve an equivalent concentration of 1.496 mL. The cultures were then grown for 24 hours. Following this step, four tubes were prepared for each serial dilution for the wild-type (WT), *Arc1*, and *Bmh1* strains. The serial dilutions were plated on YPD plates, which were then divided into two groups: treated with NaCl and untreated. The plates were incubated for 24 hours at 37°C. treated with 10 µl of 4mM NaCl and untreated which was given 10 µl ddH$_2$O in place of NaCl. The plates were incubated for 24 hours at 37°C. Strains exposed to NaCl were treated with 10 µL of a 4 mM NaCl solution. Each strain exposed to NaCl received 10 µL of the solution. The treated samples were then incubated at 37°C for 24 hours, as per standard laboratory procedures. In the control group, each strain received an equal volume of sterile water and underwent the same incubation period and temperature. All treatments and incubations were carried out in 3 rounds to ensure that the results were reproducible and accurate. Yeast growth was measured at four dilutions using ImageJ software (34). Images of the diluted samples were first converted to grayscale by changing the image type to 8-bit. Contrast was adjusted to improve the visibility of yeast colonies. Thresholding was used to isolate yeast growth regions by adjusting the threshold levels until only yeast colonies were visible. Each colony was then selected by measuring its area and recording the value.

Results

NaCl creates an external hypertonic environment, causing water to exit yeast cells and resulting in cellular dehydration and stress. This disrupts the osmotic balance within the yeast cells, leading to stress responses and reduced cell viability. The experimental procedure was designed to assess the responses of *Arc1* and *Bmh1* strains to NaCl-induced stress compared to the wild-type strain. A spot assay was conducted on different plates to determine the differences in growth between the genes (Figure 6). The results for *Arc1* showed better growth compared to *Bmh1* when incubated with the diluted NaCl solution. In contrast, *Bmh1* exhibited less growth than *Arc1* under the same conditions.

Interestingly, *Arc1* displayed growth patterns similar to the wild-type (WT) yeast strain across multiple sets of spot assays. This trend is clearly shown in Figure 7, where *Arc1* grows better than *Bmh1* when exposed to NaCl. Meanwhile, *Bmh1* demonstrated growth patterns closely mimicking the WT yeast strain in Figure 7, particularly at the 10^{-2} dilution. These observations suggest that *Arc1* plays a significant role in regulating yeast's response to osmotic stress.

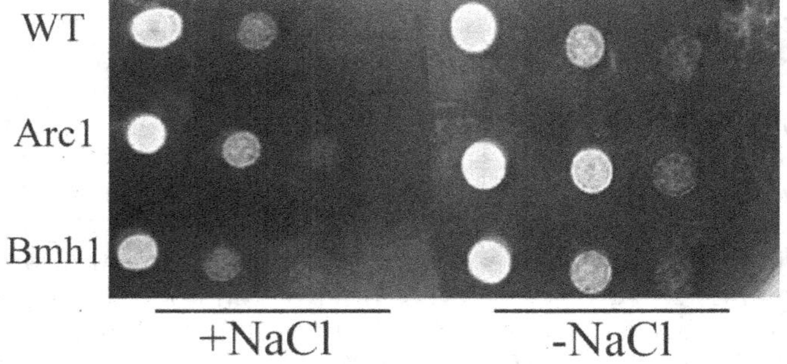

Figure 7: Spot assays of WT, ARC1 KO and BMH1 KO exposed to NaCl or unexposed to NaCl. The NaCl-exposed strains (Figure 6, left) were treated with 10 µl of 4mM NaCl and incubated for 24 hours at 37°C. The control group (Figure 6, right) was treated using water and incubated for 24 hours at 37°C.

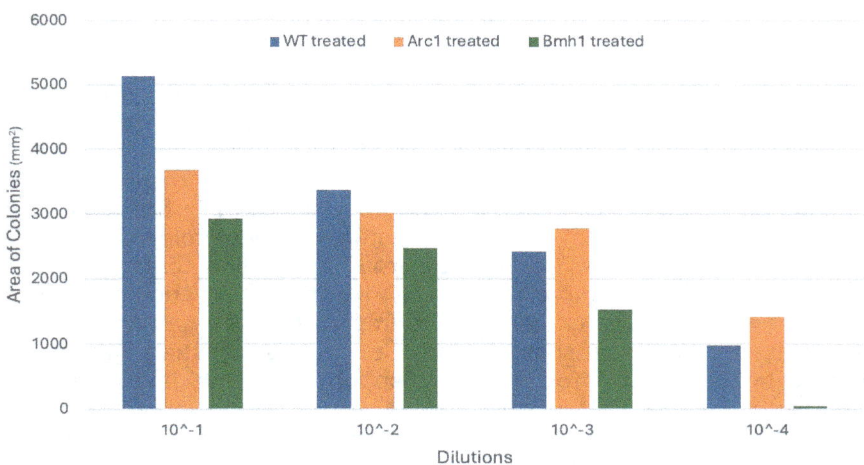

Figure 8a: Comparison of Colony Area in Various Dilutions for Yeast Strains WT, Arc1, and Bmh1 with NaCl Treatment.

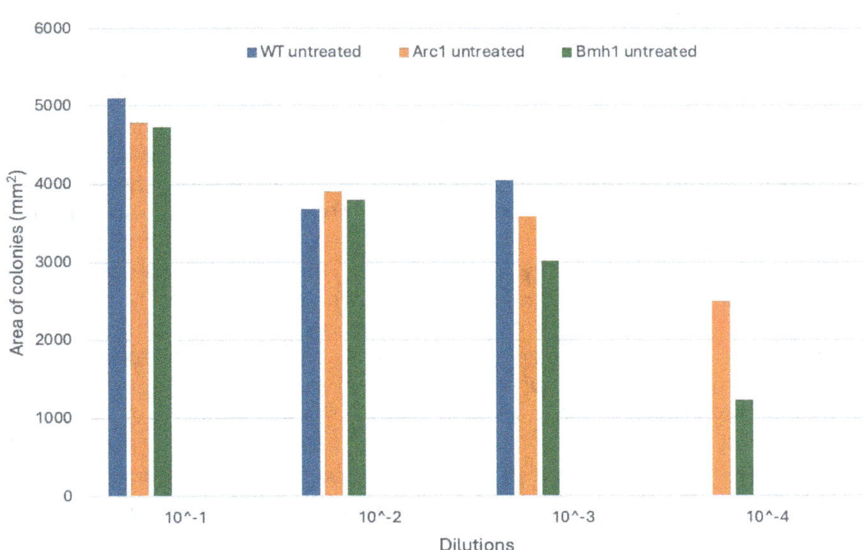

Figure 8b: Comparison of Colony Area in Various Dilutions for Yeast Strains WT, Arc1, and Bmh1 without NaCl Treatment.

Discussion

Our experimental results confirm that mutations in *Bmh1* increase the vulnerability of cells to osmotic stress caused by NaCl, leading to a stronger stress response which would lead to reduced population growth. However, mutations in *Arc1* appear to have minimal impact on cell sensitivity to the same stressor, indicating only a slight change in the stress response. These findings clarify the specific functions of *Bmh1* and *Arc1* in the yeast cell's ability to adjust to osmotic stress. Understanding these roles is crucial for comprehending how cells react to external stimuli and could potentially lead to strategies for improving stress tolerance in practical situations. The spot assay results emphasize the importance of *Arc1* in regulating how yeast populations respond to osmotic stress, suggesting that genetic modifications in *Arc1* offer promising opportunities for developing new therapeutic approaches targeting osmotic stress response pathways. This study validates that *Bmh1* mutations increase cell vulnerability to osmotic stress induced by NaCl, leading to an overexpression of these genes due to the response of *Bmh1* to osmotic stress.

Additional spot assay trials can be conducted to increase the accuracy of this data and will allow for statistical analyses of the data to determine statistical significance of the results. It is also essential to test the sensitivity of *Bmh1* and *Arc1* to different types of stress, such as oxidative stress induced by hydrogen peroxide (35). Testing cell growth with higher concentrations of sodium chloride will help determine maximum sensitivity. Notably, *Arc1* cell sensitivity responses may differ between different yeast strains and such studies would provide further insights. If the *Bmh1* gene could be cloned into a suitable plasmid, it would be possible to test rescuing *Bmh1* knockout yeast cells with *Bmh1* to rescue the phenotype, followed by determining whether the transformation activates the p53 tumor suppressor gene, which is involved in repair and response to different types of cellular damage. Overall, understanding these mechanisms enhances our comprehension of how cells manage their stress tolerance, which has practical applications in various environmental and everyday contexts.

PROJECT 4: DEVELOPING METHODS TO DETECT STRUCTURAL CHANGES IN IME2 AND SPO73 YEAST MUTANT REPRODUCTIVE STATES

This project focuses on two yeast genes: *IME2* and *SPO73*. SPO73 encodes a protein that serves to elongate the prospore membrane during sporulation in *Saccharomyces cerevisiae*, a meiotic process in which a diploid yeast cell divides into 4 haploid daughter cells. *SPO73* allows for the movement of the prospore membrane towards the nuclear envelope to envelop the products of meiosis to create spores. *SPO73* has been previously understood to be important for spore wall formation for prospore membrane expansion, as it acts as an antagonist to the bending of the prospore membrane (36). Also worth noting is that Spo73 is a dysferlin domain only protein, dysferlin being necessary in the repair of skeletal muscle and cell membranes, and may aid in research of different muscular dystrophy disorders.

IME2 on the other hand, functions as an inducer of meiosis. IME2 encodes a protein that functions as a kinase during chromosomal division to facilitate the separation of the chromosomes into two new haploid cells. *IME1* is required for the transcription of several genes relating to sporulation, including *IME2* (37).

In nutrient deficient circumstances, both genes may be activated to produce viable daughter *S. cerevisiae* cells. However it is unknown if these genes play a role in the creation of pseudohyphal growths. Pseudohyphal (or filamentous) growths are an elongated, branched, multicellular growth form of yeast produced in response to nutrient deprivation. The growths remain connected to one another and typically invade the surface of whatever media they are on, increasing their resistance to removal from the media as compared to the non-invasive form of the yeast. The goal of the experiment was to determine if the *IME2* or *SPO73* knockouts (KO) in *Saccharomyces cerevisiae*, would exhibit differences in the formation of pseudohyphal growths compared to a WT yeast under identical conditions.

Experiment and Methods

The three strains used in the study (*IME2* KO, *SPO73* KO and WT) were all mating type "alpha." These were mixed with a WT mating type "a" strain in order to form diploid pairs for the experiment.

Nutrient deficient (ND: containing 0.05% dextrose, 0.1% yeast extract and 1% potassium acetate) and nutrient rich (YPD: a standard yeast-culture media containing 2.0% dextrose, 1.0% yeast extract and 2.0% peptone) broths were created. Six tubes, three each of YPD and ND broths respectively, were prepared for three strains of yeast (WT, *IME2* KO, and *SPO73* KO) for a total of eighteen tubes. Each tube was started with 10 mL of broth and inoculated. The tubes were allowed to incubate at room temperature for 24 hours.

50 ul of broth culture from each tube was pipetted onto a glass slide and viewed under a microscope at 100X magnification. Pictures were taken using an iPhone 8 through the eyepiece.

Plates with the same composition as the tubes were also prepared. Six plates for each strain were created with the same media composition as the broth tubes, consisting of 3 ND and 3 YPD plates, for a total of 18 plates. The cultures were allowed to incubate for 24 hours at 30°C.

Cells were prepared for microscope viewing by using an inoculation loop to remove cells from the plate and added to 50 ul of distilled water, vortexed, and pipetted onto a glass slide, repeating for each of the plates. The samples were observed under the microscope at 100X magnification and photographed.

Due to possible mechanical issues with inoculation loop transfer and vortexing disruption of delicate projections, media was used to create media directly on slides by adding 75 ul of media to a glass slide, repeating the process for all 18 slides (an example is shown in figure 9). Six slides for each strain were created in the same fashion as the plates, consisting of 3 ND and 3 YPD slides. The slides were stored in Petri dishes to remain sterile, and allowed to incubate for 24 hours at 30°C. The slides were observed under a microscope at 100X magnification, and then incubate for an additional 24 hours at 30°C. The slides were observed under a microscope a second time using the same objective, and then photographed.

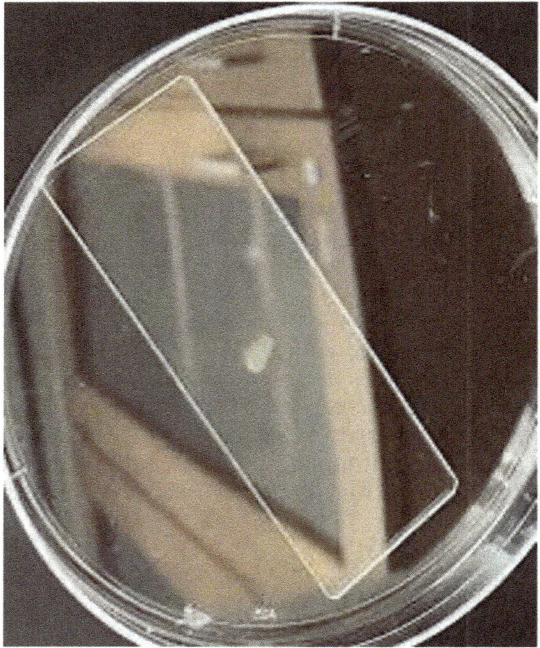

Figure 9: Slide with agar: The slide cultures were created by adding agar directly to the glass slide, and inoculating yeast directly onto the media on the slide. Pictured is an ND slide with a WT strain colony.

Results

When the *SPO73* KO was grown in ND media, we observed that the strain had similar structures to what was observed in the WT *S. cerevisiae*. When the *IME2* KO was grown in ND media, the yeast grew in a "clover" like structure which was not seen in the other strains. No pseudohyphal growths were observed in *IME2* KO or *SPO73* KO, even after a hard wash, and sporulation was not observed in either knockout. None of the growths exhibited the elongated and connected form associated with pseudohyphal growths, nor the round haploid tetrad with each spore encased in a spore wall associated with sporulation.

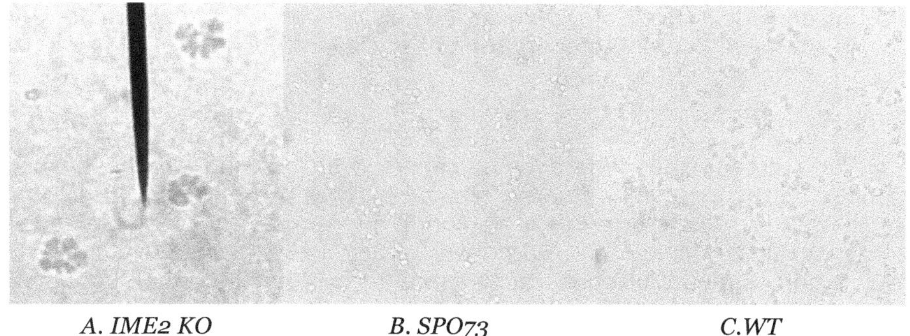

A. IME2 KO	*B. SPO73*	*C. WT*

Figure 10: IME2 *KO,* SPO73 *KO and WT yeast grown in ND media: The* SPO73 *KO strain (B) and WT (C) exhibited similar growth patterns in ND media, and were indistinguishable from one another. Neither strain underwent sporulation. The* IME2 *KO strain (A) formed abnormal structures. It is unknown if the structures are related to sporulation.*

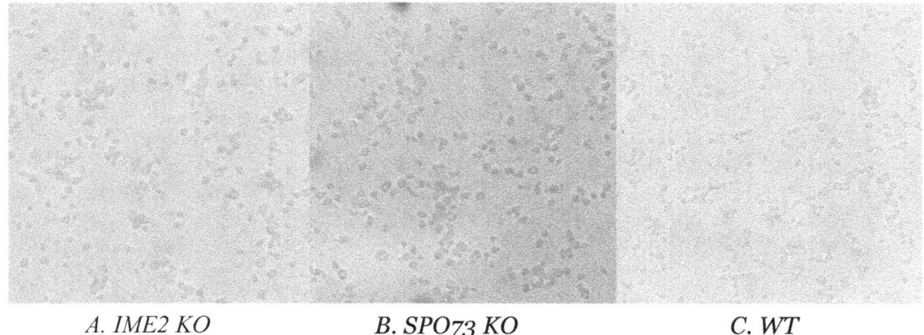

A. IME2 KO	*B. SPO73 KO*	*C. WT*

Figure 11: IME2 *KO,* SPO73 *KO and WT grown on YPD media: The* IME2 *KO strain (A),* SPO73 *KO strain (B), and WT (C) exhibited similar growth patterns in YPD media, and were indistinguishable from one another.*

Similarly, all three strains (*SPO73* KO, *IME2* KO, WT grown on YPD media (Figure 11) did not undergo sporulation or form pseudohyphal growths. Both knockouts grown on YPD media exhibited similar morphology to the WT.

For both ND and YPD groups, a single representative was selected from each of the *IME2* KO, *SPO73* KO, and WT replicates. The unpictured replicates were similar in appearance to the selected representatives.

Future experiments would focus on meiotic processes downstream of *IME2* and why the "clover" structure occurred in the *IME2* KO strain. It is also advisable to perform the same experiment with different KO strains and see if the "clovers" form. It is also necessary to determine why sporulation was not detected in any of the strains.

Conclusion

The projects proposed here were chosen from among the best work conducted this year as evaluated in a competitive presentation. As part of their work, students often develop continuing interest in these biological systems due to the extensive time which they invest in the development, realization, and troubleshooting that are all components of a successful research project. Each member of the group presenting the most highly regarded project receives small awards and the privilege of prominently displaying their project in the Biology department.

We intend to continue working on these projects, and we hope that future students may elect to build on some of the results presented here.

WORKS CITED

Angelova, M. I., Bitbol, A. F., Seigneuret, M., Staneva, G., Kodama, A., Sakuma, Y., ... & Puff, N. (2018). "pH sensing by lipids in membranes: The fundamentals of pH-driven migration, polarization and deformations of lipid bilayer assemblies." *Biochimica et Biophysica Acta (BBA)-Biomembranes, 1860*(10), 2042-2063. E. A. Winzeler et al., (1999) "Functional characterization of the *Saccharomyces cerevisiae* genome by gene deletion and parallel analysis." *Science.* 285(5429), 901-906.

Balzi, E., et al. "The Multidrug Resistance Gene PDR1 from *Saccharomyces cerevisiae.*" *J. Biol. Chem.*, vol. 262, no. 35, Dec. 1987, pp. 16871–79

Buechel, E.R. and Pinkett, H.W. (2024) "Activity of the pleiotropic drug resistance transcription factors Pdr1p and Pdr3p is modulated by binding site flanking sequences." *FEBS Lett.*, 598: 169-186.

Burbelo PD and Hall A (1995) "14-3-3 proteins. Hot numbers in signal transduction." *Curr. Biol.,* 5(2):95-6.

de Bettignies, G., Barthe, C., Morel, C., Peypouquet, M. F., Doignon, F., & Crouzet, M. (1999). "RGD1 genetically interacts with MID2 and SLG1, encoding two putative sensors for cell integrity signaling in *Saccharomyces cerevisiae.*" *Yeast,* 15(16), 1719–1731.

Fardeau, Vivienne, et al. (2006) "The Central Role of PDR1 in the Foundation of Yeast Drug Resistance." *J. Biol. Chem.,* 282(7), 5063–74.

Fujita, M., & Kinoshita, T. (2010). "Structural remodeling of GPI anchors during biosynthesis and after attachment to proteins." *FEBS Lett.,* 584(9), 1670-1677.

G. Giaever et al., (2002) "Functional profiling of the *Saccharomyces cerevisiae* genome." *Nature,* 418, 387-391.

Guttmann-Raviv, Noga, et al. (2002) "Ime2, a Meiosis-Specific Kinase in Yeast, Is Required for Destabilization of Its Transcriptional Activator, Ime1." *Mol. Cell. Biol.,* 22(7), 2047–56.

Hong, S., Lee, H. G., & Huh, W. K. (2024). "ARV1 deficiency induces lipid bilayer stress and enhances rDNA stability by activating the unfolded protein response in *Saccharomyces cerevisiae.*" *J. Biol. Chem.,* 300(5).

Karabinos, A., et al. (2022). "Dilated cardiomyopathy is a part of the ARV1-associated phenotype: a case report" *J. Med. Case Rep.,* 16(1), 98.

Kaster, K. R., Burgett, S. G., & Ingolia, T. D. (1984, July). Hygromycin B resistance as domaint selectable marker in yeast. *Curremt Genetics, 8,* 353-357.

Kolaczkowski M, Kolaczowska A, Luczynski J, Witek S, Goffeau A. (1998) "In vivo characterization of the drug resistance profile of the major ABC transporters and other components of the yeast pleiotropic drug resistance network." *Microb Drug Resist.,* 4(3):143-58.

MacPherson S, Larochelle M, Turcotte B. (2006) "A fungal family of transcriptional regulators: the zinc cluster proteins." *Microbiol Mol Biol Rev.,* 70(3):583-604.

Mahé, Y., Parle-McDermott, A., Nourani, A., Delahodde, A., Lamprecht, A., & Kuchler, K. (1996). "The ATP-binding cassette multidrug transporter Snq2 of *Saccharomyces cerevisiae*: a novel target for the transcription factors Pdr1 and Pdr3." *Mol. Microbiol.,* 20(1):109-17.

Mahilkar, A., Nagendra, P., & Saini, S. (2022). Determination of the Mating Efficiency of Haploids in Saccharomyces cerevisiae. Journal of visualized experiments : JoVE, (190), 10.3791/64596.

Molk, J. N., & Bloom, K. (2006). "Microtubule dynamics in the budding yeast mating pathway." *J. Cell Sci.*, 119(17), 3485–3490.

Nolan S, Cowan AE, Koppel DE, Jin H, Grote E. (2006) "FUS1 regulates the opening and expansion of fusion pores between mating yeast". *Mol Biol Cell.*, 17(5):2439-50.

Obsilova V, Obsil T. (2024) "The yeast 14-3-3 proteins Bmh1 and Bmh2 regulate key signaling pathways." *Front Mol. Biosci.*, 11:1327014.

Okai, H., et al (2020). "Cold-sensitive phenotypes of a yeast null mutant of ARV1 support its role as a GPI flippase." *FEBS Lett.*, 594(15), 2431-2439.

Okumura, Yuuya, et al. (2016) "The Dysferlin Domain-Only Protein, Spo73, Is Required for Prospore Membrane Extension in *Saccharomyces cerevisiae*." *MSphere*, 1(1):e00038-15.

Plasencia, I., Norlén, L., & Bagatolli, L. A. (2007). "Direct visualization of lipid domains in human skin stratum corneum's lipid membranes: effect of pH and temperature." Biophysical journal, 93(9), 3142-3155.

Schneider, C. A., Rasband, W. S., & Eliceiri, K. W. (2012). "NIH Image to ImageJ: 25 years of image analysis". *Nat. Meth.*, 9(7), 671-675.

Segel, R., et al (2020). "A defect in GPI synthesis as a suggested mechanism for the role of ARV1 in intellectual disability and seizures." Neurogenetics, 21, 259-267.

Shcherbakova, P., & Pavlov, Y. (1993). "Mutagenic specificity of the base analog 6-N-hydroxylaminopurine in the URA3 gene of the yeast *Saccharomyces cerevisiae*." *Mutagenesis*, 8 5, 417-21.

Shimada, Yoshihiro et al. (2023) "Spermiogenesis in *Caenorhabditis elegans*: An Excellent Model to Explore the Molecular Basis for Sperm Activation." *Biomolecules,* 13(4) 657.

Simos G, et al. (1998) "A conserved domain within Arc1p delivers tRNA to aminoacyl-tRNA synthetases." Mol. Cell 1(2):235-42.

Simos G, et al. (1996) "The yeast protein Arc1p binds to tRNA and functions as a cofactor for the methionyl- and glutamyl-tRNA synthetases." *EMBO J,* 15(19):5437-48.

Tinkelenberg, A. H., Liu, Y., Alcantara, F., Khan, S., Guo, Z., Bard, M., & Sturley, S. L. (2000). "Mutations in yeast ARV1 alter intracellular sterol distribution and are complemented by human ARV1." *J. Biol. Chem.*, 275(52), 40667-40670.

Tkach JM, et al. (2012) "Dissecting DNA damage response pathways by analysing protein localization and abundance changes during DNA replication stress." *Nat. Cell Biol.*, 14(9):966-76.

Tong, F., et al (2010). "Decreased expression of ARV1 results in cholesterol retention in the endoplasmic reticulum and abnormal bile acid metabolism." *J. Biol. Chem.*, *285*(44), 33632-33641.

Tran, K. and Green, E. M. (2019) "Assessing Yeast Cell Survival Following Hydrogen Peroxide Exposure." *Bio-protocol,* 9(2): e3149.

Villasmil, M. L., Ansbach, A., & Nickels Jr, J. T. (2011). "The putative lipid transporter, Arv1, is required for activating pheromone-induced MAP kinase signaling in *Saccharomyces cerevisiae*". *Genetics*, 187(2), 455-465.

Wach, A., Brachat, A., Poehlmann, R., Philippsen, P. (1994) "New heterologous modules for classical or PCR-based gene disruptions in *Saccharomyces cerevisiae*." *Yeast*, 10(13), 1793-1808.

White JM, Rose MD. (2001) "Yeast mating: getting close to membrane merger". *Curr Biol.*, 11(1):R16-20.

Wong ED, Miyasato SR, Aleksander S, Karra K, Nash RS, Skrzypek MS, Weng S, Engel SR, Cherry JM (2023) "Saccharomyces genome database update: server architecture, pan-genome nomenclature, and external resources." *Genetics*, 224(1).

Carbon Capture: Investigating Carbon Dioxide Removal via Chemical Reaction

By **Trinit'y Mitchell**
Sponsored by **Rita K. Upmacis, Ph.D.**
Chemistry and Physical Sciences, New York

ABSTRACT

Anthropogenic carbon dioxide (CO_2) emissions, primarily from fossil fuel combustion, transportation, and industrial processes, are driving global climate change. Post-combustion CO_2 capture technologies, particularly those utilizing amine-based compounds, have shown promise in reducing emissions from commercial plants. However, their implementation is hindered by high installation and maintenance costs. This study aims to explore novel CO_2 capture mechanisms by investigating the interactions between metal-ammine compounds, formally known as Werner Complexes, and various forms of CO_2 in different solvents. Werner complexes, including hexaamminecobalt(III) chloride and hexaammineruthenium(III) chloride, were reacted with aqueous forms of CO_2 (bicarbonate and carbonate). The resulting compounds were crystallized and characterized using X-ray crystallography. The study led to the generation of compounds bearing bound forms of CO_2. This research enhanced our understanding of CO_2 reactions with metal-ammine complexes and identified favorable conditions for CO_2 binding. Future work in this area may potentially contribute to the development of more efficient and cost-effective carbon capture technologies.

INTRODUCTION

Anthropogenic carbon dioxide (CO_2) emissions are leading to global climate change, and it is necessary for technologies to be developed that enable carbon capture and its storage for later usage. A primary source of anthropogenic CO_2 emissions is from the combustion of fossil fuels for energy (e.g., power plants). Significant quantities of CO_2 emissions are also produced by our use of transportation and by the industrial sector as a by-product in the generation of consumer goods from raw materials. In response, Carbon Capture Utilization and Storage (CCUS) technologies, particularly post-combustion CO_2 capture techniques, have been identified as strategies that reduce CO_2 emissions (Dubey et al., 2022). Gases are produced from commercial plants and then these are scrubbed to remove the CO_2 from entering the atmosphere.

By 2016, it was reported that more than 30 commercial plants have been constructed that are capturing the CO_2 from gaseous emissions (Richelle, 2016). The largest plant is a power plant based in Lubbock, Texas, which can strip up to 1,100 tons of CO_2 gas per day from waste gas (U.S. Department of Energy, 2024). Commercial Power plants implementing CCUS technologies offer a beacon of hope for large-scale carbon mitigation; however, the financial and technical barriers associated with this technology highlight the need for continued research and development to identify more efficient and cost-effective solutions (Medlock et al., 2021).

The only technology that is being seriously considered for CO_2 scrubbing from the exhaust of coal- and gas-fired power plants involves the use of various types of compounds containing amine substituents ($-NH_2$), such as that found in the substance, monoethanolamine ($HOCH_2CH_2NH_2$) (Richelle, 2016). The reaction relies on the amine portion of the substance reacting with CO_2 to facilitate its capture. Importantly, the reaction is reversible at high temperature, such that the CO_2 can be released and stored elsewhere or used in a subsequent process that requires this form of carbon. However, this technology is not widely implemented because of the expense involved in its installation and maintenance. There is also the question of how much CO_2 can be extracted using this amine. Monoethanolamine has a low absorption rate of CO_2 and requires specific conditions to extract even small amounts (Hack, 2022).

Emerging research has begun to explore the potential of the ocean as a natural sink for CO_2, leveraging its vast capacity to absorb and store carbon. Direct air capture (DAC) offers another solution to high emissions released into the atmosphere. Utilizing the DAC method would allow researchers to take 16 to 30 billion tons of CO_2 from the atmosphere in a few decarbonization scenarios (Salas, 2020). If indeed carbon was taken directly from the atmosphere, it would be considered an advantage. A large disadvantage of absorbing CO_2 in this way is the low yield of carbon collected. Another disadvantage is the high oxidative thermal stability that would need to be involved in order for DAC to work at one hundred percent (Park, 2022).

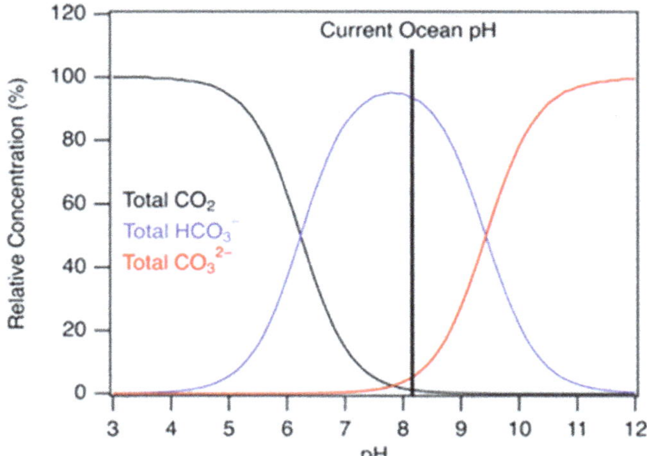

Figure 1: Relative concentrations of CO2, HCO3-, and CO3^{2-} as a function of pH.

Figure 1 is a Bjerrum plot, which is a graph that shows the speciation of dissolved inorganic carbon (as CO_2, HCO_3^-, and CO_3^{2-}) in seawater as a function of pH (Dickson et al., 2010). As can be seen on the graph, as the amount of bicarbonate increases, the total amount of carbon dioxide and carbonate ion decreases at pH 8. The carbonate ion is at its maximum intensity when the pH of the seawater is more basic, but the opposite can be seen for carbon dioxide. When carbon emissions increase in the air, the pH of the shallow ocean becomes lower than that of the deep ocean thus leading to acidification (Park, 2022). Acidification causes a lot of damage to wildlife and ocean ecosystems. When carbon is captured by the ocean, it is transformed through the ocean's ability to control the partial pressure in the atmosphere, pH and alkalinity (Park, 2022). To begin the process of carbon intake in the ocean's natural sink, alkalinity would need to be increased. Adding calcium(II) and magnesium(II) ions to increase alkalinity and reduce acidity does not affect the ecosystem (Park, 2022). Potential issues of placing minerals into the ocean include (i) adding excessive amounts such that the alkalinity is increased too much and (ii) the possibility of dissolving unwanted species or contaminants into the ocean.

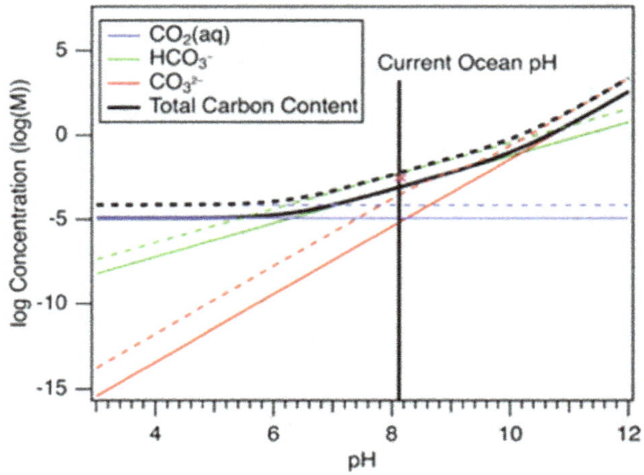

Figure 2: CO2 , HCO3-, and CO3²⁻, log concentration as a function of pH with an asterisk denoting the total carbon content collected in the ocean at 8 pH.

Figure 2 shows the CO_2 speciation vs. pH for pure water and seawater at fixed partial pressures in an open CO_2 system where the red asterisk (on the line at pH 8) denotes the total carbon content of water that is calculated (Dickson et al., 2010). It has been found that the use of carbonic anhydrase catalyzes the reversible conversion of CO_2 and water into bicarbonate which can then be sequestered by magnesium (Mg^{2+}) or calcium (Ca^{2+}) ions.

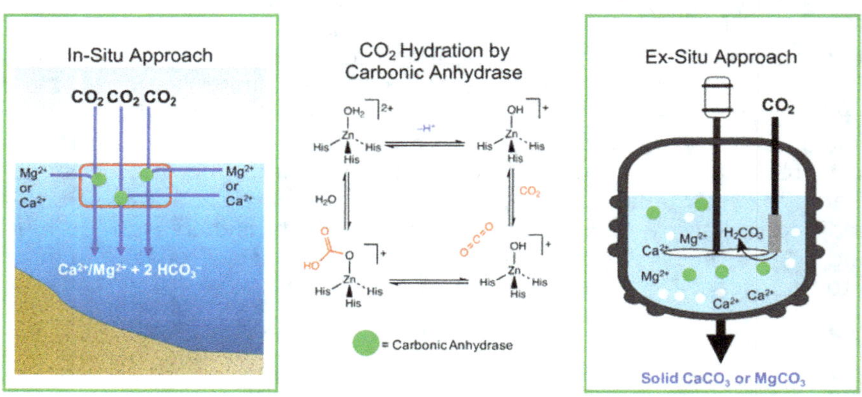

Figure 3: CO2 binds to the Ca2+ and Mg2+ metals with both in-situ and ex-situ approaches.

Figure 3 describes how CO_2 binds to the Ca^{2+} and Mg^{2+} metals with both *in-situ* and *ex-situ* approaches.

Although this may seem like an easy solution to the mineral dissolution methods, the long-term stability hinders the acceptance of this plan. There is not a specific way to know how to contain and control these substances enough to manipulate the minerals in the ocean, and further work is necessary to make it more efficient. However, molecules with copper or nickel centers provide a better way to capture the CO_2, most notably with zinc cyclen, which is a small molecule that can behave like carbonic anhydrase, acting as a catalyst to chemically capture carbon (Floyd et al., 2013).

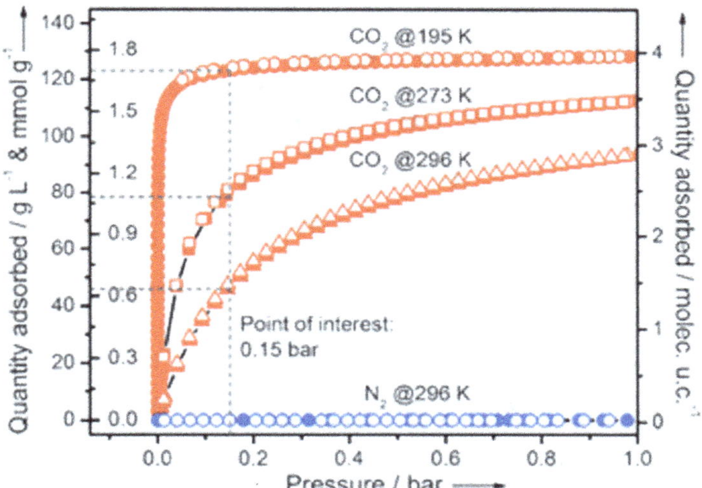

Figure 4: Gas adsorption of CO2 and N2 in isotherms using PCN-200 as the type of MOF metal organic compound, shown at deferent temperatures. The diagram shows CO2 at 195 K (red circles), 273 K (rectangles), 296 K (triangles) and N2 at 296 K (blue circles). The filled and open symbols represent adsorption and desorption, respectively, and the gray dashed lines indicate the adsorption values at 0.15 bar (partial pressure of CO2 in flue gas with typical composition of 14–16% CO2 and 75% N2) (Wriedt, 2012).

The graph in Figure 4 shows gas adsorption isotherms for CO_2 and N_2 of PCN-200 (Wriedt, 2012). The porous coordination network, PCN-200, is used for capturing CO_2. Metal-organic frameworks (MOFS) contain metal ions coordinated to these porous networks (Gurusamy, 2021). MOFs have been used to selectively capture CO_2 from power plant emissions, which is less energy intensive, while simultaneously reducing carbon emissions.

Figure 4 shows the absorption rates of CO_2 and N_2 into a metal-organic compound at different temperatures, this essentially gives insight into how metal complexes work within reactions that require the absorption of CO_2. The graph shows that it does require specific conditions to work at full capacity. The utilization of amine-based solvents for CO_2 capture represents one of the most researched and implemented methods, with compounds such as monoethanolamine playing a central role in the capture process due to their ability to react with CO_2 and form reversible bonds (Luis, 2016). Creating reversable bonds allows for release, storage or utilization of CO_2, offering a viable pathway to reducing the carbon intensity of industrial emissions.

Additionally, the exploration of metal-ammine complexes for CO_2 capture introduces a novel research avenue, aiming to uncover the mechanisms of CO_2 interaction with Werner complexes in various solvents. This line of inquiry not only expands the scope of potential carbon capture solutions but also aligns with the broader objective of identifying sustainable and economically viable technologies to combat climate change.

This project aimed to contribute to the ongoing discourse on carbon capture and storage, offering insights into potential pathways forward in the global effort to mitigate climate change.

METHODS

It was necessary to perform extensive research to identify the proper solvents to dissolve the metal compound, hexamminecobalt(III)chloride. In an article titled *"Hexaamminecobalt(III)–4-hydroxybenzene sulfonate–chloride–water"*, hexaamminecobalt(III) chloride (0.5g, 0.0018 mol) was dissolved in hot water (15 mL) with a magnetic stirring rod. In another beaker, sodium 4-hydroxybenzenesulfonate dihydrate (1.3 g, 0.0056 mmol) was dissolved in hot water (20 mL). Both solutions were then mixed and cooled to room temperature. After 2 hours, orange crystals of hexaamminecobalt(III)–4-hydroxybenzene sulfonate–chloride–water were formed, which were then filtered and air dried (Sharma et al., 2006). In another article, titled *"Second-sphere coordination complex via hydrogen bonding: Synthesis, characterization, X-ray crystal structure determination and packing of hexaamminecobalt(III) chloride di(para-nitrobenzoate),"* it was discussed that when hexaaminecobalt(III) chloride reacts with a sodium salt of *para*-nitrobenzoate in hot water, the resulting crystalline structure was identified as hexaamminecobalt(III) chloride di(para-nitrobenzoate).

Further analysis using single-crystal X-ray crystallography revealed that this structure contains the hexaamminecobalt(III) cation ($[Co(NH_3)_6]^{3+}$) and mixed anions that are held together through electrostatic forces that are attracted through second sphere coordination and hydrogen bonds (Sharma et al., 2006). Their synthesis began with $[Co(NH_3)_6]Cl_3$, already prepared *via* air oxidation of the Co(II) salt in an ammoniacal solution in the presence of activated charcoal as a catalyst. Hexaamminecobalt(III) chloride (1.00g, 0.0037mol) was dissolved in hot water (25 mL) in a beaker with a stirring rod. In another beaker, the sodium salt para-nitrobenzoate was prepared by dissolving of sodium hydroxide (0.452g, 0.0112 mol) and para-nitrobenzoic acid (1.88g, 0.0112 mol) in hot water. Both solutions were cooled, leading to the precipitation of a yellow solid. The precipitate was immediately washed with ice-cold water and allowed to air dry. Orange-yellow crystals were obtained from the hot aqueous medium which were filtered and air dried.

With what information was gathered, I based the synthesis of my carbon capturing metal-ammine complex on these previous methods with some modifications regarding the metal compounds, ligands and solvents involved.

MATERIALS USED IN THIS RESEARCH

In this study, the interactions between metal-ammine complexes and carbonate species were investigated. Hexamminecobalt(III) chloride (0.0669 g) and hexamine $Ru(III)Cl_3$ (0.0774 g) were selected as the metal-ammine complexes, with masses adjusted based on ligand molar ratios. Sodium bicarbonate ($NaHCO_3$) and sodium carbonate (Na_2CO_3) served as the source of CO_2. *Table 1* summarizes the experiments.

When the reactions were performed between hexamminecobalt(III) chloride and $NaHCO_3$, the bicarbonate was first dissolved in deionized water (1 mL) in a glass vial. The bicarbonate solution was pipetted into a second vial containing the metal-ammine dissolved in deionized water (2 mL). The mixture was gently swirled to ensure homogeneity. The vial was sealed with parafilm, which was subsequently punctured with a small needle to facilitate slow evaporation of water and potential crystal formation. This procedure was repeated for the reaction of hexamminecobalt(III) chloride with Na_2CO_3 as the source of CO_2. The entire process was then replicated using hexaammineruthenium(III) chloride as the metal-ammine complex and $NaHCO_3$ or Na_2CO_3 as a source of CO_2. All vials were appropriately labeled and left undisturbed to allow for potential crystal growth over several days. Any promising crystals were taken to the X-ray crystallography facility at Columbia University.

RESULTS AND OBSERVATIONS

Exp. No.	Date	Metal compound	Ligand	Solvent	Observations
TDM. 010	2/23/24	Hexaammine-Cobalt (III) Chloride Mw- 267.48g/mol Grams- 0.0669g	$NaHCO_3$ Mw-84 g/mol Grams- 0.084g	H_2O	3 days later: huge red/brown crystal
TDM. 011	2/23/24	Hexaammine-Cobalt (III) Chloride Mw-267.48g/mol Grams- 0.0669g	Na_2CO_3 Mw- 106 g/mol Grams- 0.1072g	H_2O	Immediate small particles look like crystals
TDM. 012	3/07/24	Hexaammine Ru(III)Cl3 Mw- 309.61g/mol Grams-0.0774g	$NaHCO_3$ Mw-84 g/mol Grams – 0.0843g	H_2O	Color was translucent at first but then increasingly became more yellow Next day: turned black
TDM. 013	3/07/24	Hexaammine Ru(III)Cl3 Mw- 309.61g/mol Grams- 0.0774g	Na_2CO_3 Mw- 106 g/mol Grams – 0.1064g	H_2O	Color was translucent at first but then increasingly became more yellow Next day: turned black

Table 1: Logged representation of the days in the lab including observations. The first column labeled Exp. No. (Experiment Number) has the initials TDM and the experiment number. The following columns include the dates, name of the metal compound used, the molecular weight (MW) in mols and grams, the ligand names, solvent, and observations.

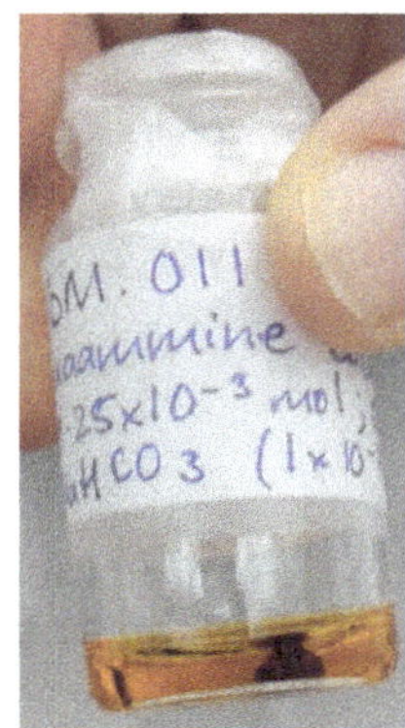

Image 1: Small dark red/ brown crystal formed when hexaamminecobalt(III) chloride (0.0669g) reacted with sodium carbonate (0.1072g).

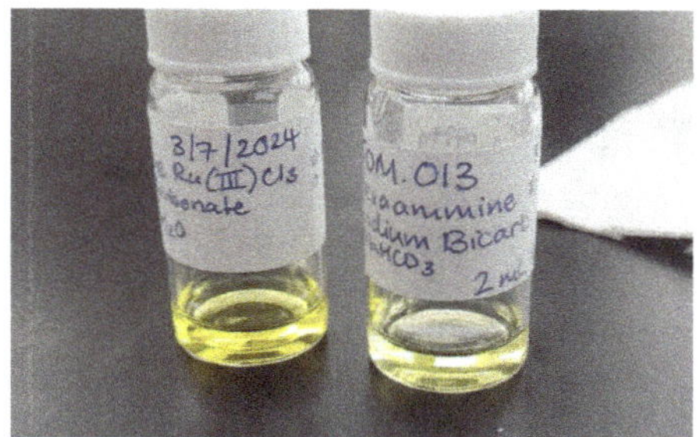

Image 2: Experiment TDM.012 shows the resulting solution when hexaammineruthenium(III) chloride (0.0774g) is mixed with sodium bicarbonate (0.0843g). Experiment TDM.013 shows the resulting solution when hexaammineruthenium(III) chloride (0.0774g) is mixed with sodium bicarbonate (0.1064g).

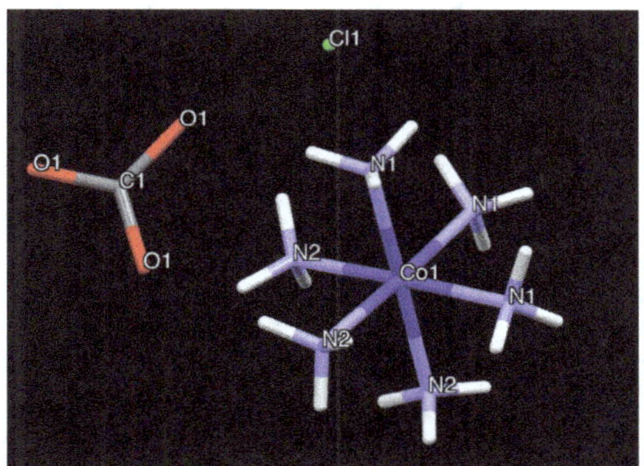

Image 3: This is a 3D image of the crystal that was collected from TDM011. This crystal formed during the reaction of hexaamminecolbalt(III) chloride (0.0669) and sodium carbonate (0.1072g).

In the quest to explore efficient carbon capture mechanisms, a series of experiments were designed to evaluate the efficacy of various ligands and metal-ammine complexes in sequestering CO_2.

The reaction between hexaamminecobalt(III) chloride and $NaHCO_3$ led to the formation of a large crystal, shown in *Image 1*. The aqueous solution in the vial is orange and at the bottom a small dark red/brown crystal has formed. The success of this investigation can be highlighted by the analysis of sample TDM.011, which was examined at Columbia University.

Image 2 shows experiments TDM.012 and TDM.013, where hexaamineruthenium(III) chloride was mixed with $NaHCO_3$ (on the right) and Na_2CO_3 (on the left). Experiments TDM.012 and TDM.013 did not yield any crystals, and interestingly, after a day, the mixtures solidified and turned black. A reaction occurred, likely a polymerization reaction, but the nature of the resulting product remains unknown. These experiments highlight the importance in the choice of the metal in the metal-hexaammine complex.

The X-ray structure of the crystal (from *Image 1*) is shown in *Image 3* (using the application, Mercury). In this image, the hexaamminecobalt(III) unit is observed, with cobalt (Co-1; dark purple) in the center bound to 6 nitrogen atoms (N-1 and N-2; light purple) of the ammine groups, forming an octahedral structure. In addition, one can also observe the carbonate unit represented by carbon (C-1; grey) attached to 3 oxygen atoms (O-1; red). There is also a chlorine counterion (Cl-1, green). Hydrogen-bonding between the oxygen atoms of the carbonate and the hydrogen atoms of the ammine groups (O•••H), as well as a Cl•••H hydrogen-bonding function to stabilize this structure in the crystalline state. During research, we found that the structure has recently been published (Pyrch et al., 2022). Through the collaboration with Dr. Upmacis, this research showcases how CO_2 attaches to the metal in the form of a carbonate, CO_3^{2-}.

DISCUSSION

This pivotal discovery highlights the conversion of the carbonate to its elemental carbon form to facilitate effective carbon capture. It was during this phase of research that the work of Mikaela Mary F. Pyrch et al., titled *"Investigations of the Cobalt Hexaammine Uranyl Carbonate System: Understanding the Influence of Charge and Hydrogen Bonding on the Modification of Vibrational Modes in Uranyl Compounds,"* was discovered, which showed that our structure had been previously published. This published article also shed light on the crystallization of uranyl tricarbonate complexes with hexamminecobalt(III) chloride. The analytical journey through experiment TDM.011 affirmed the potential of metal-ammine complexes in carbon capture. The choice of metal-ammine compound used proved to be critical to the outcome, revealing that not all metal-ammine complexes behave uniformly; rather, their efficacy in CO_2 capture vary, highlighting the unique nature of each compound's interaction with CO_2. This overlap not only validated our experimental approach but also highlighted the scientific community's concerted efforts towards understanding and enhancing carbon capture technologies.

CONCLUSION

Studying the different methods of carbon sequestration stresses the subtle role of ligands and metal-ammine complexes for capturing CO_2 through chemical reactions. The results from this research indicate the potential use of these complexes in environmental remediation efforts to enhance carbon capture efficiency, although further studies would be required. The use of hexamminecobalt(III) chloride demonstrated how it can be used to capture CO_2 in the form of CO_3^{2-}. The choice of metal (cobalt or ruthenium) affected our results, suggesting that optimized carbon sequestration technologies require a detailed understanding of the chemistry involved and the underlying mechanisms. While further research is required, the results from our study reaffirm the value of exploring various ligands and metal-ammine complexes as viable pathways for CO_2 sequestration. These insights offer a promising outlook for the future of environmental preservation and climate change mitigation, contributing to the broader scientific endeavor to develop effective solutions to environmental challenges.

WORKS CITED

Dickson A. G ; Riebesell U., Fabry V. J., Hansson L., and Gattuso J-P. (Editors) (2010). Part 1: Sewater carbonate chemistry (Luxembourg: Publications Office of the European Union). [12] Bjerrum J., McReynold J. P., Inorg. Synth. 2 (1946) 216.

Dubley, A., Arora A., "Advancements in Carbon Capture Technologies: A Review." *Journal of Cleaner Production*, Elsevier, 1 Sept. 2022, www.sciencedirect.com/science/article/abs/pii/S0959652622035041.

Floyd, W, et al. "Evaluation of a Carbonic Anhydrase Mimic for Industrial Carbon Capture." *ACS Publications: Chemistry Journals, Books, and References Published ...*, pubs.acs.org/doi/abs/10.1021/cen-09418-notw12. Accessed 15 Sept. 2024.

G. T. Richelle, "3- Conventional amine scrubbing for CO_2 Capture" from Absorption-Based Post-Combustion Capture of Carbon Dioxide, 2016, 35-67, http://dx.doi.org/10.1016/B978-0-08-100514-9.00003-2.

Gurusamy, L., and J. Wu. "Metal Organic Framework." *Metal Organic Framework - an Overview | ScienceDirect Topics*, www.sciencedirect.com/topics/chemistry/metal-organic^sframework#:~:text=MOFs%20(metal%2Dorganic%20frameworks),porous%20%5B1%E2%80%935%5D. Accessed 14 Sept. 2024.

Hack J, M. N, M. DM. Review on CO_2 Capture Using Amine-Functionalized Materials. ACS Omega. 2022 Oct 28;7(44):39520-39530. doi: 10.1021/acsomega.2c03385. PMID: 36385890; PMCID: PMC9647976.

Luis, P., Use of monoethanolamine (MEA) for CO_2 capture in a global scenario: Consequences and alternatives, Desalination,Volume 380, 2016, Pages 93-99, ISSN 0011-9164, https://doi.org/10.1016/j.desal.2015.08.004, (https://www.sciencedirect.com/science/article/pii/S001191641500418X).

Medlock, K., and Miller K. *Expanding Carbon Capture in Texas.* Rice University's Baker Institute, 2021, https://www.bakerinstitute.org/sites/default/files/2022-09/expanding-ccus-in-texas.pdf. Accessed 13 Sept. 2024.

Park A-HA and Vibbert HB. Harvesting, storing, and converting carbon from the ocean to create a new carbon economy: Challenges and opportunities. 2022 Front. Energy Res. 10:999307. doi: 10.3389/fenrg.2022.999307.

Pyrch, M., Bjorklund J., Williams J., Kasperski M., Mason S., Forbes T., "Investigations of the Cobalt Hexamine Uranyl Carbonate System: Understanding the Influence of Charge and Hydrogen Bonding on the Modification of Vibrational Modes in Uranyl Compounds." *Inorganic Chemistry*, 2022, 61, 15023-15036.

Salas, J. "The Future of Carbon Capture." *The Aspen Institute*, 10 Sept. 2020, www.aspeninstitute.org/blog-posts/the-future-of-carbon-capture/.

Sharma, Raj Pal et al. "Hexaamminecobalt(III)–4-Hydroxybenzenesulfonate–Chloride–Water (3/8/1/13)." Metal Organic Papers, *Acta Crystallographica Section E, Structure Reports*, 2006, E62, m2113-m2115.

Sharma, R.P., Bala R., Sharma R., Perez J., Miguel D., "Second-sphere coordination complex via hydrogen bonding: Synthesis, characterization, X-ray crystal structure determination and packing of hexaamminecobalt(III) chloride di(para-nitrobenzoate)," Journal of Molecular Structure, Volume 797, Issues 1–3, 2006, Pages 49-55, ISSN 0022-2860, https://doi.org/10.1016/j.molstruc.2006.03.046.

U.S Department of Energy, Office of Scientific and Technical information, OSTI.gov "Waste CO_2 Supports Three Texas EOR Projects." *Well Serv.;* OSTI.com, www.osti.gov/biblio/5953259. Accessed 5 Apr. 2024. https://www.osti.gov/biblio/5953259.

Wriedt, M., J. P. S., Andrey A. Yakovenko, Yuguang Ma, Gregory J. Halder, and a. H.-C. Z. Perla B. Balbuena Low-Energy Selective Capture of Carbon Dioxide by a Pre-designed Elastic Single-Molecule Trap. 2012, 5 DOI: 10.1002/anie.201202992.

Immigration Reform and the Labor Market: Examining *SB1070*'s Wage Implications

By **Anastasia Khanukov**
Sponsored by **Mary Kaltenberg, Ph.D.**
Economics, New York

ABSTRACT

This study investigates the economic ramifications of Arizona's *SB1070* on the wages of local residents within the state. The controversial immigration policy, which was enacted in April 2010, gave law enforcement the authority to inquire about individuals' immigration status. As undocumented workers were targeted, with many forced to leave the state, a debate began on the subject regarding the wages of residents and the impacts on the labor market. Using preliminary findings from various sources, including data from the U.S. Census Bureau, allows for a multitude of quantitative analyses. Specifically, the Difference-in-Differences model framework aids this study in evaluating the effectiveness of *SB1070* on the labor market, both before and after the policy implementation. Comparing the effects on wages in Arizona, to New Mexico, provides empirical insight into immigration policy discourse and dynamics within the labor market. The results show that the policy implementation impacted wages mostly in a negative way, with non-citizens still making less than citizens.

INTRODUCTION

This paper focuses on undocumented workers and residents living in the states of Arizona and New Mexico. Similar to previous works, I analyzed data in both states and counties, to differentiate the wage implications on the residents of Arizona, who were impacted by *SB1070* in 2010. The purpose of this paper is to suggest that policies targeting undocumented workers may not cause an upward trend in wages for other residents in the state. Many factors are taken into consideration, such as employment status, educational attainment, and citizenship status. Previous papers have used data from the United States Census (e.g. Gaynor, 2017), which was also done in this study, with the help of data extraction from IPUMS. By observing over 300,000 individuals within the years 2006 to 2015, this paper compares the before and after effects of *SB1070*, using a difference-in-differences model, with OLS estimation, to observe the parallel trends and changes. Incorporating fixed effects within the panel data decreased endogeneity, by controlling for any time-varying factors within (e.g. national macroeconomic conditions, global economic trends).

This difference-in-differences model, using OLS estimation, concluded that the decrease in undocumented workers may have created a decrease in wages and income for the majority of the population within Arizona. Moreover, with the incorporation of counties bordering Mexico, the percentage of wages fell among residents. The OLS estimation suggests that there was more statistical significance within certain groups than others, alluding to the fact that other immigrant groups and races were impacted.

As this paper will break down the found estimations and results, it is organized with a literature review focusing on previous works surrounding immigration and policy effects, continued with data and methodology, followed by the summation of results. Lastly, as this study focuses primarily on immigration law and labor economics – policy recommendations and further suggestions are included in the conclusion.

LITERATURE REVIEW

Immigration Background

To control the number of undocumented workers within the state of Arizona, policy *SB1070* was passed in 2010, also known as one of the strictest anti-illegal immigration laws in the United States (Hoekstra & Orozco-Aleman, 2017). With the help of recent data, it shows that there are nearly eleven million undocumented immigrants living in the United States, as of 2023 (Passel & Krogstad, 2023). Similarly, in the time-period in which the policy was enacted (2010), there were 11.2 million undocumented immigrants residing within the U.S (Pew Research Center, 2011). To control the rate of illegal immigration, many policies have been adopted. As the most common country of birth for unauthorized immigrants is Mexico, bordering states such as Arizona implemented *SB1070* (Passel & Krogstad, 2023). Other states began to create copycat laws,[1] such as Alabama, Georgia, and Indiana (Wang, 2012). The actual policy, *SB1070,* had bias factors, such as allowing law enforcement to approach individuals they deemed as "illegal," charging those who were assisting and hiring undocumented workers, and seeking out undocumented individuals in public areas (e.g. schools and daycare programs). Due to the profiling done by law enforcement and the dangerous bias surrounding undocumented workers, the policy became very controversial. Therefore, it went to the Supreme Court in 2012, with *Arizona v. United States* (Torre, 2012).

---

1 Copycat laws were deemed as 'unconstitutional' along with *SB1070*, due to the enforcement causing an infringement on human rights. By encouraging law enforcement to label individuals by their looks, many have argued that such policies have made the state(s) more harmful and biased (Wang, 2012).

As immigration rates continue to rise globally, it is essential to study policy implications and the effect on labor markets. In the United States alone, the migrant population rose by about 1.6 million between 2016 and 2021. Recent estimates show that with the rise of environmental issues and humanitarian crises, this number will only grow (Lundh & Shepperson, 2023). With the help of previous literature and research, examining the effects of undocumented workers within various regions in the United States has been possible. Much of the existing research has focused on immigration reform, starting with population numbers and ending with the effects of local wages (Sanchez 2017, Piyapromdee 2021). Many papers have used U.S Census Data but also surveyed undocumented workers themselves, to emphasize the fear and rationale that policy changes create within their environment (Sadowski-Smith & Wei Li, 2006).

Effects on Population

In previous literature, topics surrounding immigration have been studied thoroughly, using various types of methodologies and data sets. A recurring theme amongst recent works has been to use data extracted from United States surveys, such as *CPS* (Current Population Survey) and *ACS* (American Community Surveys). Using the previous work of Peri (2014), who incorporated various countries within their methodologies (e.g. U.S., Canada, Germany), this study will also focus on U.S. census microdata to focus primarily on one nation. Moreover, incorporating a 'county' variable will highlight the U.S-Mexico border, where a large population of undocumented workers resides. Variables used within past works are incorporated within this paper to ensure full variety and characteristic inclusion.

An important factor in studying the implications of Arizona *SB1070* comes with understanding the population within the research premises. This can be done by looking at immigrants based on their personal experiences through conducting interviews. From the works of Smith and Li (2016), interviewees from several countries, such as Russia and the United States were included to create a comparison of experiencing anti-immigrant sentiment. Following the theory of economic migration, it was proven that although they felt targeted, migrants still acclimated to the environment rather than leaving. As mentioned by Valdez, Valentine, and Padilla (2013), 96% of the interviewees were undocumented immigrants, who had resilience and optimism for living in the United States – hence supporting their willingness to stay in the country. However, being targeted addresses the persistent stress and displacement that these populations dealt with during anti-immigration policy implementations. Understanding the motivation to stay in such a high-risk environment conforms to the work of this paper, as it is essential to note population changes, due to the impact on wages. In addition, it is important to address the legislation history within such policies, as it correlates with the number of immigrants residing within a state. As mentioned in the works of Wallace (2014), there is statistical significance among wages and the states that introduce similar legislation to *SB1070* versus those that do not. However, there is only a 3% shift in Latino populations between such states, supporting the fact that legislation does not correspond to immediate emigration. In correlation to this working paper, integrating anti-immigration policy laws will present implications on the labor market, which supports the current hypothesis. To facilitate new research, comparative legislation such as *Alabama HB56*[2] may be referenced to compare the effects of *SB1070*, or even the updated policy *SB1379*.

Economic Theory

The economic theory following supply and demand has shaped the research done regarding adjusted income and wages within local economies. For example, the supply of immigrants has been compared to the demand needed by firms within a labor market. Due to the controversial topic of immigration within the United States, it is pivotal to show the effects of such populations on the local economy. Chassamboulli and Peri (2015) address demand theory, proving that policies aimed at reducing undocumented workers will reduce the job creation of firms and increase the unemployment of unskilled resident workers. As this can directly affect the wages of residing populations, it is pivotal to incorporate it within this future research. As there are 11 million undocumented immigrants residing in the United States, there is a significant amount of labor force participation. Referencing the work of Borjas (2017), it has been proven that the wages of undocumented workers are 23% less than citizens, and 17% below legal immigrants. When looking at the wages of individuals around the age of 45, previous literature has shown immense growth in the wage gap between citizens and non-citizens. To prove this, Borjas (2017) incorporated cross-sectional analysis to measure wage evolution. Although cross-sectional data is often used in previous works, it may cause possible errors and limitations, as it does not account for time effects or endogeneity induced by individual differences. This is due to personal characteristics that may impact an individual's work, so it is essential to use gender, skill level, experience, and educational attainment to obtain future results while incorporating time-fixed effects.

As wages are the main point of study within my research, incorporating longer-year terms and a different data set (U.S Census Data) would add to the previous numbers and show more diversity, such as addressing the female undocumented population. As noted by Piyapromdee (2021),

---

2 This policy was implemented in 2011 and was labeled as one of the harshest immigration laws, following Arizona *SB1070*. The law allowed for individuals to be arrested under "suspicion" of how they looked, identical to the biased implications of *SB1070 (Zhang, Palma, Xu, 2016)*.

taking these characteristics into account shows specific labor force characteristics, such as in 2007 when there were 3.6 million new high-skilled immigrants and 4.6 new low-skilled immigrants. It is important to note that the level of skill an individual has is based on their educational attainment and schooling years. As these factors are key to *SB1070*, and copycat policies, it would allow for future research to derive the exact impact of low-skilled versus high-skilled workers and answer the question of wage fluctuation on residing populations. In the work of Gaynor (2017), it has been shown that the short-term wage effects of immigrants are close to zero, and that immigrants boost productivity in wages within the long run. If policies such as *SB1070* lower wages for the local sector, it is essential to account for years prior and the after-effects to measure by how much. Within this new research, variables of prior literature will be used, but interactions amongst variables (e.g. citizenship and Hispanic) will be included to add further information.

The theory following supply and demand clearly states that an increase in the supply of labor can potentially impact wages. Furthermore, with human capital theory, the skill level of immigrants, relating to the existing workforce, influences the overall productivity and economic impact of immigration. The hypothesis is that, by *SB1070* being enacted, residents may not see a positive shift in their income and wages. As Borjas (2017) mentioned, undocumented workers throughout their prime years of work (30-50) make significantly less than U.S. citizens, even with 92% of undocumented men being employed, along with 61% of undocumented women. As immigration numbers are on the rise, this study considers previous policy effects and implications to show the productivity of migrants, state employment levels, and categorical data.

SB1070 AND IMMIGRATION POLICY

Policies such as *SB1070* are developed due to the argument that jobs and wages are affected with the rise of immigration. As undocumented workers join the labor force, politicians are expecting to see a negative trend in civilian incomes and productivity within markets and firms. In reference to the human capital theory, it is essential to note the characteristics that construct and create an advantageous worker. When labeling an individual as a "skilled worker," it is by their education level and quality, training, and even attitude toward their career (Acemoglu & Pischke, 2009). Therefore, the theory suggests that well-paid employees tend to have an upper hand in the job market, due to continued training and prior educational attainment (Engbom, 2022). With this concept, the discussion surrounding undocumented workers becomes controversial due to many being labeled as "unskilled workers." It is not because they are not capable of such endeavors but because their backgrounds did not allow for proper schooling and training.[3] Therefore, the overall economic impact of immigrants is mostly based on their skills and background–rather than the mere fact of entering the workforce. However, with the causal reasoning of policies such as *SB1070*, it may become difficult to advance undocumented workers within their career sectors in the United States.

In reference to Figure 1, between the years 2006 and 2015, non-citizens in the United States were making less in income and wages. As this is measured in Arizona and New Mexico, it can be noted that the percent rate of income continues to fall for non-citizens, in comparison to citizens. However, individuals who were born outside of the United States but had at least one parent to sign for their citizenship, made the most. Hence, this can be explained by the human capital theory, as it relates to the implementation of prior resources that can lead to the advancement of an

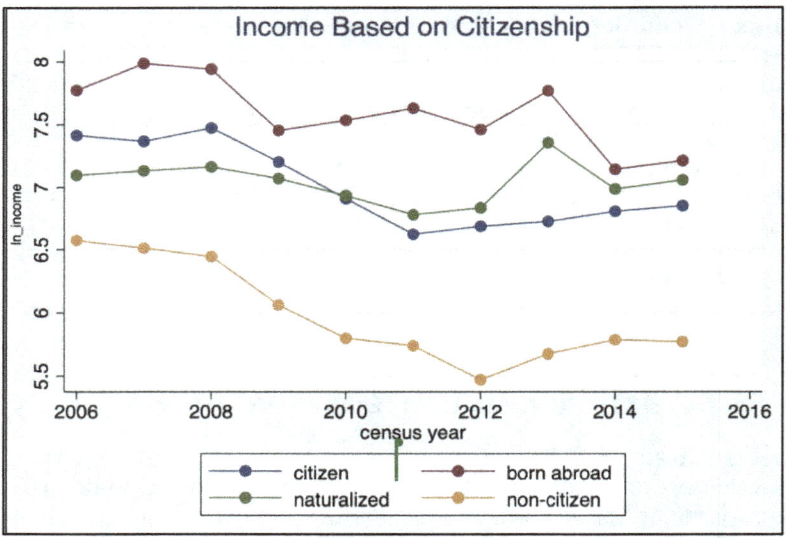

Figure 1: Percentages of Income Based on Citizenship Status, Arizona & New Mexico, 2006-2015

individual. It can be proven here that oftentimes; non-citizens do not have the abundance of materials that other groups within the United States do. However, regarding naturalized citizens and citizens born in the United States, there was a similar trend between the percentage of income and

3 Many jobs and firms provide basic training, but rarely pay for additional advancements that could lead to a salary raise and further compensation. Thus, being counter-productive to the development of the labor market at times (Acemoglu & Pischke, 2009).

wages in the two states. This could be explained by outside factors[4] that are not studied within this paper.

The additional theory of supply and demand must be included to emphasize the economic narrative surrounding labor markets. As the participants within a labor market are workers and firms, undocumented workers may potentially impact wages (Card, 1990). However, the abundance of individuals migrating to the United States provides essential roles in entrepreneurship, by creating job vacancies and a greater number of firms (Azoulay, 2022). Therefore, there are larger opportunities for economic growth within U.S. markets and higher[5] positions. As mentioned earlier, human capital is essential to identify whether an individual is considered skilled or unskilled, which correlates with supply and demand. Although there are greater numbers of undocumented workers, the specific job they can "take" is based on the skill level of the individual, rather than them just entering the workforce. On the other hand, policies such as Arizona *SB1070* were pushed to create a greater barrier within the labor market; and to create greater supply for unskilled local workers. Both

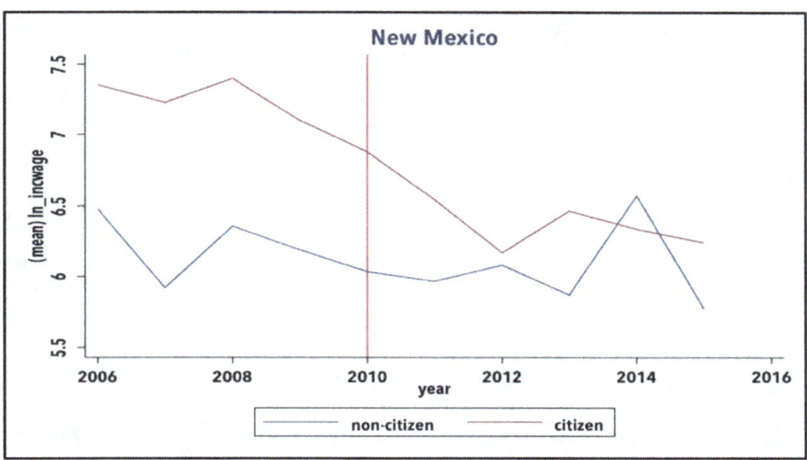

*Figure 2: Percentage of Income by Citizenship Status,
New Mexico, 2006-2015*

---

4 It is important to note that there may be macroeconomic and global trends that affect the wages and incomes of individuals. The suggestion of a downwards trend after 2008, could be the causal impact of the mortgage crisis and other economic events. Between October 2008 and April of 2009, an estimate of 700,000 Americans lost their jobs (The Hamilton Project, 2011).

5 Many undocumented workers take on positions that U.S.-born citizens and naturalized citizens tend to avoid due to specialization and resource abundance. Such industries include but are not limited to agriculture, mining, and construction (Edwards & Ortega, 2016).

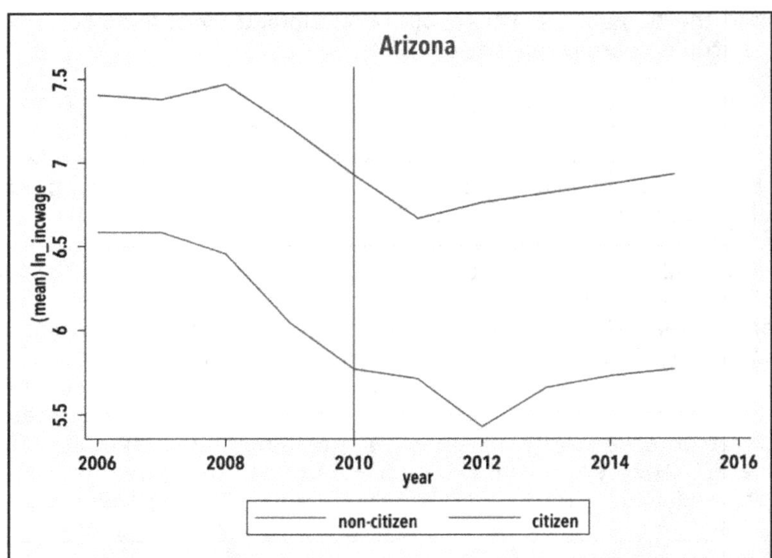

*Figure 3: Percentage of Income by Citizenship Status,
Arizona, 2006-2015*

economic theories create the framework of this paper, by allowing for prior concepts to predict the effects that *SB1070* had on Arizona and its labor market. Thus, the hypothesis results in the assumption that *SB1070* may not influence the income and wages of those residing in the state.

To further extend this idea, reference Figures 2 and 3, where New Mexico and Arizona are compared side-by-side. This is done to differentiate the incomes of non-citizens and citizens through the years of 2010-2015 individually, as both states have different GDPs and employment rates. It is clear that in the state of New Mexico in 2010 (the policy implementation year), citizens were seeing a drastic drop in wages. Moreover, a similar trend was occurring in Arizona around the year 2010, although the state's GDP and wages are much higher. However, within the population of non-citizens, in both states, there is a negative trend within the group, as it is steadily much lower than the citizens residing within the state. But, in 2012 in New Mexico, both groups were very close to having a similar trend in wages. Many factors could have contributed to the economy and wages of the two population groups, but it is clear that non-citizens still drastically make much less[6] than the average U.S. citizen.

---

6 Non-citizens make less than the average U.S Citizen in all years, except for in New Mexico during the 2014 time-period.

DATA AND METHODOLOGY

The data for this paper was extracted from *IPUMS*, which is an integrated, publicly used microdata series. This database collects its information from a range of agencies, including the *Census Bureau*, the *Bureau of Labor Statistics*, and the *National Science Foundation*. With over 300,000 individuals within the dataset, this larger sample size reduces error and provides mass representation. The range of years chosen was 2006 to 2015 to emphasize the pre and post-periods of *SB1070*, with 2010 being the year the policy was enacted. As there are multiple regressions within this paper, a wide range of variables are included to try to ward off omitted variable bias while strengthening the foundational economic theories. Due to limitations with the data available for representing the number of undocumented workers, other variables have been implemented to properly characterize and group the population. Sanchez (2017) and Lozano (2015) found that adding variables such as *Hispanic Origin*, *Citizenship Status*, and *Educational Attainment* have contributed to the methodology, as these characteristics tend to represent undocumented workers. Within this paper, similar variables are implemented to adhere to the available data and avoid selection bias. Moreover, various methods have been configured within this research topic, such as incorporating OLS estimation methods, regression models, and comparing cross-sectional data. In the previous works of Peri (2014) and Gaynor (2017) cross-sectional data and panel analysis were incorporated to support the static model of labor demand and supply. Rather than using data from two separate years, 2009 and 2012, this current study will focus on the years 2006 through 2015, to avoid errors in calculating effects on wages.

Table 1 includes the list of variables, with the proper numerical results of the means, standard deviations, and minimum and maximum qualities. It is important to note that categorical variables (e.g. *Race, Age, Gender*) are made into percentages, in order to see the size of the population group within the dataset. As income and wages are being tested for, it is a logged variable to emphasize the percentage change amongst the specific period (2006-2015). Moreover, as Arizona and New Mexico are different-sized states, the *logged GDPs* and *Unemployment Rate*s are included to try to remove the economic biases. Furthermore, with this research surrounding the labor climate in both states, *Employed* (employment status) was added, as the effects on income may depend on such a qualifier. Regarding the previous mention of the human capital theory, various *Educational* levels (educational attainment) represent the individual being labeled as 'skilled' or 'unskilled,' hence the need for defining their level of education. In addition, as it is difficult to find data on undocumented workers, various *Citizenship* statuses were added to characterize those residing and working within the states of Arizona and New Mexico. The same was done with the *Hispanic* (origin) variable, to include the large population that resides within both states, as they border Mexico. Moreover, *Bordering* (counties) are included for counties which border Mexico, as they have a much larger migrant population coming from Mexico as well. The counties in which data was collected can be referred to in Figure 4, with some bordering the country of Mexico.

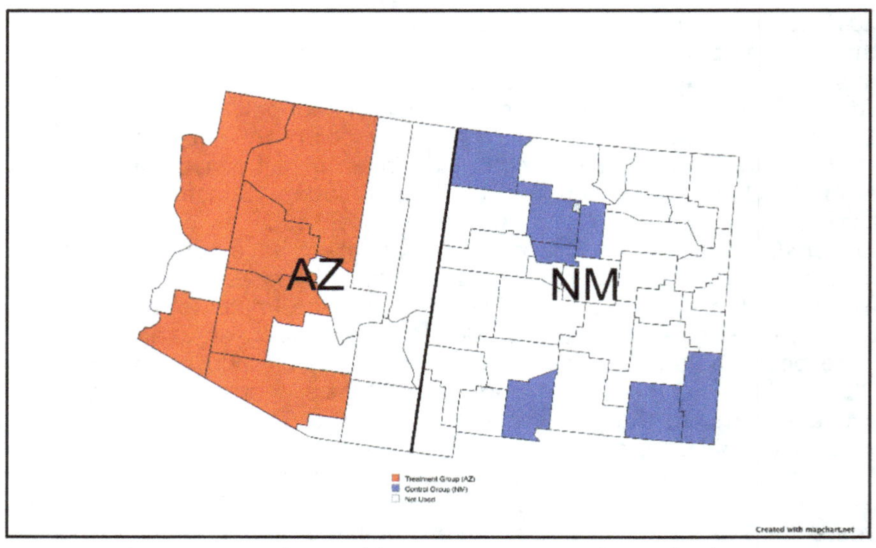

Figure 4: Counties Used in Dataset, New Mexico and Arizona

Categorical variables are essential to gain insight into specific groups of individuals, their characteristics, and what makes them unique in comparison to others. Hence, this paper includes variables such as *Race*, *Gender*, and even *Age*. Such categories are essential for this study, as these characteristics may impact the income and wages of an individual, merely based on immutable factors. However, *Age* being a numerical value that is ever-changing, hence it is included, as incomes change over time, specifically in this panel dataset. Moreover, within previous literature, it was an essential variable used to test for the wage gap in various periods, between undocumented and documented workers (e.g. Borjas, 2017). *Race* was also broken apart by percentage groups, to further stress the different representation that was presented within the dataset collected from IPUMS.

(1) Summary Statistics

	Mean	Standard Deviation	Minimum	Maximum
Ln_Incwage	6.913975	4.814742	0	12.91657
Ln_GDP	12.38118	.3680652	11.36278	12.55409
Unemployment Rate	7.104214	2.101702	3.591667	10.3
State	1.118272	.3229305	1	2
Citizen	90.05%	.2992778	0	1
Not a Citizen	9.95%	.4947113	0	0
Age	44	14.97808	18	70
Gender (Male)	.4874799	.4998439	0	1
White	80.07%	2.180152	0	1
Native American	4.07%	.1977425	0	1
African American	3.50%	.1837991	0	1
Chinese	0.68%	.0824359	0	1
Japanese	0.18%	.0424538	0	1
Other Races	11.5%	.2537465	0	1
Attainment: College	55.8%	.3397822	0	1
Attainment: High School	41.05%	.2137160	0	1
No Schooling	0.96%	.0979669	0	1
Hispanic Origin	26.1%	.4396723	0	1
Employed	64.82%	.4775098	0	1
Not in Labor Market	30.04%	.4584581	0	1
Unemployed	5.14%	.2205441	0	1
Bordering Counties	77.49%	.4176256	0	1
N Total	394,886			
N Arizona	348,182			
N New Mexico	46,704			

Table 1: Variables, Means, Standard Deviations, Minimums, Maximums

As the methodology of this paper uses a two-time period difference-in-differences model, it allows for the comparison of the pre-policy years and those after. Due to this, the variable *SB1070* was created to account for all counties that had the policy implemented, versus those that did not. By taking *SB1070* and interacting it with the variable *year*, it represented the counties that had the policy enacted, along with the years of the implementation.[7] This way, it became possible to show the difference between incomes in both states over the specific time period. Moreover, *YearSBCitizen,* a triple interaction, tested for the significance of the years and counties for when the policy was present, and its effects on income and wages on specific citizenship attainments.

---

7 The variable *yearsb* was created by this interaction, which was used as the treatment group. The variable covered all the counties affected by the policy in Arizona, during the years of the policy implementation.

With the use of these variables, it became possible to use the difference-in-differences model and OLS estimation to compare the effects of *SB1070* throughout 2006 and 2015, whilst running regressions using *STATA*. To control for unobserved time-specific factors, time-fixed effects are used in the base model of this study, and the additional two robustness check models. Incorporating time-fixed effects in the regressions allows for the models to account for time-constant heterogeneity that may come across the dataset. Moreover, to account for the possibility of heteroscedasticity, cluster robust standard errors at the individual level are used in the regression analysis. To represent the first empirical approach, the following equation was used:

$$LnIncwage_{it} = B_0 + B_1 Citizenship_t + B_2 Empstat_t + B_3 Hispanic_i + B_4 Male_i + B_5 Race_i + B_5 State_i$$
$$+ B_6 UnemploymentRate_t + B_7 LnGDP_t + \delta_{DD}(Year_i * SB1070_t) + \omega t + e_{it}$$

In the base model, *LnIncwage* is the dependent variable, which this study is testing for, in state *i* in time of *t*. With income and wages being logged, this will make the coefficients represent a percent change in relation to the other variables. The key variable in this base model is the treatment interaction of *Year* and *SB1070*, which is the control, as it compares when the policy was implemented to which select area (Arizona). The categorical variables present the differences among the individuals in the dataset, showing those that were impacted by the policy more. *Male* represents a binary variable used in the dataset (male, female), in addition to the *Race* variable ranging from *White, Black, Asian*, etc. With the number of undocumented workers being a difficult number to estimate, *Citizenship* implied various levels of attainment, such as U.S.-born citizens, naturalized citizens, and those who were born abroad with American parent(s). Moreover, the categorical variable of *Hispanic* represents individuals who are not Hispanic, or are either Mexican, Puerto Rican, etc. Since employment status may impact wages significantly, *Empstat* was used to measure how an individual was represented in the labor market, as either unemployed, employed, or not in the labor force. Moreover, as the *States* differ in population and economic factors, *UnemploymentRate* and *LnGDP* were included to account for such disparities. Additionally, time-fixed effects () are included, along with the error term (to account for factors that are not explicitly included.

The second regression model looks the same, but it includes "if Border = 1", which means that it is comparing the data to bordering versus not bordering counties. By including this in the analysis, it serves to show the percentage change of income and wages in bordering counties, whilst being in the affected counties within the year the policy was enacted. As the bordering counties may have a much larger migrant population, this regression can show more of a difference amongst wages in citizen vs.

non-citizen groups. This is a robustness check that merely incorporates the *Border* variable within the regression. Again, time-fixed effects () are included, along with an error term (. The second model is presented as shown:

$$LnIncwage_{it} = B_0 + B_1 Citizenship_t + B_2 Empstat_t + B_3 Hispanic_i + B_4 Male_i + B_5 Race_i + B_5 State_i$$
$$+ B_6 UnemploymentRate_t + B_7 LnGDP_t + \delta_{DD}(Year_i * SB1070_t) + \omega t + e_{it}$$

Lastly, a robustness check is used to account for those individuals who are employed, in comparison to those who are not, with the use of "if Employment = 1" whilst running the regression. As the focus of the research study continues to be on logged income and wages (*LnIncwage*), more interactions are included to compare differences. *Year*, *SB1070*, and *Citizenship* are all interacted to make one variable, to compare individuals who are citizens vs. non-citizens in the time of the policy enactment in Arizona. In addition, the *Year* and *SB1070* interaction is still included, to measure the wage difference separately, in comparison to employed and non-employed individuals. An error term (is essential, along with the time-fixed effects (), thus being added again. Adding the additional variables resembles the third model:

$$LnIncwage_{it} = B_0 + B_1 Citizenship_t + B_2 Hispanic_i + B_3 Male_i + B_4 Race_i + B_5 UnemploymentRate_t$$
$$+ B_6 LnGDP_t + \delta_{DD}(Year_i * SB1070_t) + \delta_{DD}(Year_i * SB1070_t * Citizenship_t) + \omega t + e_{it}$$

RESULTS

In reference to Table 2, by running the first base-model regression, it may be concluded that the original hypothesis could be correct. The results of the statistically significant variable *YearSB* show that in 2010, the year of the policy implementation, in the affected Arizona counties, there was about a *9.57%* decrease in income and wages for individuals residing within the state. This is in comparison to the years in which *SB1070* was not enacted yet in the unaffected counties in New Mexico. Similar to the graphs presented in the paper, it is clear that *Citizens* make a larger income, with about a *57.5%* positive change. Moreover, the binary gender variable shows that during this time period, males were making about *28.8%* more than females. The results adhere to the impacts of employment on wages, by showcasing a very large negative trend for those that are *Unemployed*. *Race*[8] has statistical significance within the regression, as various categories of individuals represent diverse results. With a sample size of 394,886, the results in 64.6%, adhering to the fact that the variance in the dependent variable (*LnIncwage*) is explained by the independent variables within the model.

---

8 The most statistically significant races impacted by the policy were individuals who are Chinese (46% increase), and those who are two major races (17% increase).

With respect to the second regression, the treatment variable, *YearSB,* resulted in being statistically insignificant. This could be due to the fact that the regression specifically focuses on bordering counties, which the data has a lack of. Thus, it cannot be said that the hypothesis was proven or disproven within this regression, but there are still variables that show to be statistically significant. For example, it is found that *Citizens* still make more than non-citizens, with an increase of about *57.1%* in income and wages. Moreover, similar to the first regression, males are shown to be making *32.9%* more than females in counties bordering Mexico. *Race*[9] also shows to be statistically significant in this regression, with all groups seeing an increase in their incomes. As only bordering counties are considered in this regression (in comparison to non-bordering counties) the sample size is 88,875 with an of 63.4%.

In the third regression, *YearSB* was statistically significant when looking at the employed population within the dataset. It shows that citizens who were employed during the time of policy implementation in Arizona, saw about a *20.6%*[10] decrease in their wages (in comparison to the control group). Moreover, with the *YearSB* and *Citizenship* interaction, it is made evident that citizens who are employed make about *21%* more in comparison to non-citizens who are. This goes back to the human capital theory, where it states that unskilled versus skilled workers have a significant difference in income, due to *Educational Attainment.* In comparison to the previous two regressions, males are still making more than females during this time period, with about a *26.7%* increase in wages and income. The only *Race* group that shows to be statistically significant is those who are *Chinese,* with about a *41.1%* increase in wages for those who are employed. As only individuals who are *Employed* are represented in this regression, the sample size comes out to be 255,994 with an of 1.2%. As the is extremely low, it can be said that the independent variables are not adding value to this particular model and lacking representation for the dependent variable.

---

9 African Americans (25.5% increase), Chinese (43.1% increase), Japanese (13.8% increase), and White (17.5% increase).

10 As this percentage only represents employed versus unemployed people, the percent change may be much bigger.

	(1) ln_incwage	(2) ln_incwage	(3) ln_incwage
ln_GDP	-0.796** (-13.92)	0.564 (0.44)	1.726 (3.16)
Unemployment Rate	-0.0324** (-21.17)	-0.0203 (-0.89)	0.0199 (2.25)
Citizen	0.575*** (141.51)	0.571*** (117.16)	0.617* (11.66)
Years	-0.0598* (-9.74)	-0.0805 (-1.19)	-0.0251 (-0.90)
YearSB	-0.0957*** (-87.76)	-0.0736 (-2.98)	-0.206** (-18.17)
Male	0.288*** (88.90)	0.329** (22.93)	0.267*** (272.38)
African American	0.164 (4.21)	0.255** (48.69)	0.106 (4.04)
Chinese	0.461** (36.82)	0.431** (27.75)	0.411*** (96.67)
Japanese	0.259 (4.46)	0.138** (32.67)	0.151 (2.50)
Two Races	0.173** (56.30)	0.142 (2.13)	-0.0464 (-1.21)
White	0.178 (5.79)	0.175** (36.19)	0.0508 (3.98)
Hispanic	-0.156* (-7.64)	-0.0839 (-4.74)	-0.193 (-4.40)
Unemployed	-4.805*** (-103.71)	-4.741*** (-119.70)	X
Citizenship#YearSB	X	X	0.211* (7.91)
_cons	19.06** (24.81)	1.960 (0.12)	-12.49 (-1.85)
N	394,886	88,875	255,994
R^2	0.646	0.634	0.012
adj. R^2	0.646	0.634	0.012

t statistics in parentheses
* $p < 0.10$, ** $p < 0.05$, *** $p < 0.01$

Table 2: SB1070's Wage Implications: Fixed Effects Panel Estimation

DISCUSSION

To come by the regression results in Table 2, it was essential to use time-fixed effects, to adhere to unobserved time-specific factors. Moreover, as all regressions are using panel data, from the years of 2006-2015, it was essential to account for outside factors that could shift the results. Furthermore, to account for the possibility of heteroskedasticity, robust standard errors are used in every regression, to account for idiosyncratic errors. With the majority of the empirical results, it is proven that the original hypothesis may be correct. The implementation of *SB1070* in 2010, played a large role in the wages of individuals in Arizona state. Again, this is in comparison to New Mexico, where the policy implementation never took place.

As the difference-in-differences model is used throughout this study, a parallel trends graph was conducted to further examine the implications of the policy. In reference to Figure 2, it is shown that after the policy was enacted in 2010, residents in Arizona saw a decrease in wages, in comparison to those in New Mexico. However, it is important to note that the GDP and population of Arizona are much larger than New Mexico.

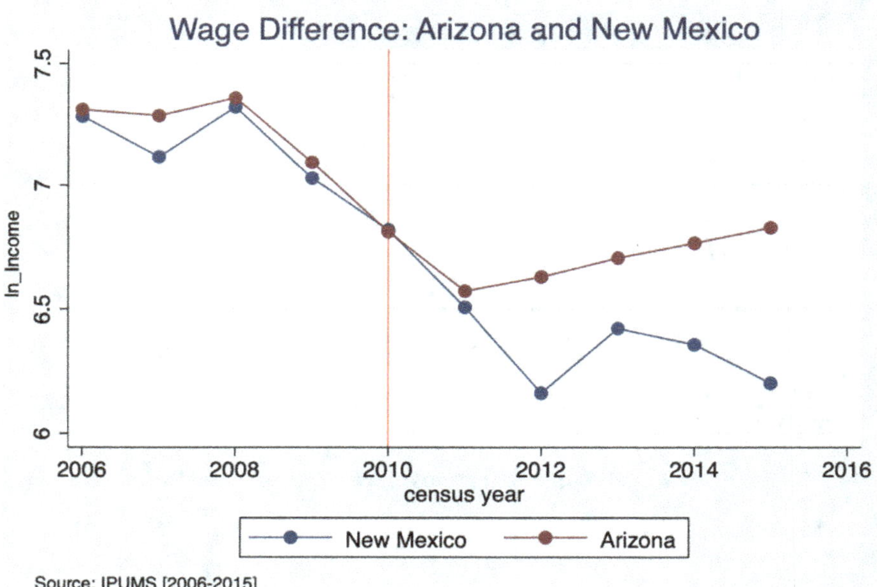

Figure 5: Parallel Trends of Income by State, Arizona & New Mexico, 2006-2015

CONCLUSION

With the assistance of previous studies and literature, the goal of this paper was to prove that such policies would not create a positive trend in the wages of individuals within the Arizona region. Luckily, with the use of *IPUMS* data and over 300,000 observations, the empirical results supported the original hypothesis. In Tables 1 and 2, it was essential to account for various categories and groups of people, as the dataset was massive and provided enough information to do so. Similarly, within prior literature, there was statistical significance among a range of variables (Wallace, 2014).

After *SB1070* was implemented, it became clear that wages went down, due to the fear in the migrant population (Sadowski-Smith & Wei Li, 2006). As many were forced to leave and emigrate to other regions in the United States, there was a shift created within the labor market. Therefore, the regression results in Table 2 go against the argument of the policymakers, in reference to the residents living in Arizona having a disadvantage within the labor force. This was further proven by the results due to the negative wage implications the policy had on *non-citizens* and those of *Hispanic* origin, even before the policies were enacted. By having the migrants fear work and residency, it created a negative wage trend for the U.S. citizens working and living in Arizona during the policy implementation.

In accordance with human capital theory, it is essential to note that more skill and scholarship an individual may have, is correlated with the amount of money that they are making. Hence, undocumented workers are oftentimes considered "unskilled workers," due to the lack of resources they have available to them in their home countries (Chassamboulli & Peri, 2015). This may explain the reason as to why their income levels continuously fell in relation to the other individuals within the study. In the results, it was common to see the individuals who are *unemployed*, or *not in the labor force*, have negative income trends, in comparison to those who have jobs.

As this paper references the labor market in regards to undocumented workers, the focus was moved to *Border* counties within the second regression. As Arizona and New Mexico border Mexico, the presumption was that the policy implementation occurred due to the greater population of undocumented individuals. It was evident that *Citizens* were still making more than *non-citizens*, even in bordering counties. However, it is essential to note that *YearSB* saw no statistical significance. This could have been due to the fact that the sample size was much smaller than the original regression model and the dataset lacked information for all border counties. In future research it would be essential to add more *bordering* counties and implement the rest of the *non-bordering* counties amongst both states (for an informative sample size and comparison).

Although there is not a positive correlation between income and wages for residents of Arizona, due to the policy implementation, a lot of bias and fear spread within migrant communities. This was seen as many emigrated away from the state of Arizona, even if it was temporary (Valdez, Valentine & Padilla, 2013). Moreover, studies show that as undocumented workers joined the labor force, it created more room for newer firms to open, with diverse jobs becoming available to the public (Peri, 2014). These individuals have been proven to absorb themselves in any job market while becoming compliments to the other workers around them (Peri, 2014). By initiating policies such as *SB1070*, immigrants are forced to leave their jobs, creating job vacancies that the general public will most likely not take.[11] Rather than trying to keep the undocumented workers out, policies should be enacted to assist them once they arrive in the United States, due to the ongoing conflicts occurring in their home countries. In the case of Arizona, *SB1070* did not have a "benefit" to income and wages, as many migrants refused to go back to their home countries and traveled back[12] to the state (Sanchez, 2017).

In summation, it is clear that this anti-immigration policy did not benefit the people residing within Arizona, as most groups saw a decrease in their wages. As the low-skilled undocumented workers left various industries, it was difficult to find substitutes and replacements amongst the citizen population, thus leading to a downward trend within income rates. In the future, there are many areas to expand on within this paper. Although there were efforts used to avoid heteroskedasticity and various biases, omitted variable bias may still be present. As mentioned earlier, it is difficult to gather precise data on the number of undocumented workers that reside within an area, so certain variables are used to try to group individuals. In addition, other variables can be incorporated within the regressions, such as the skill-specific wages, bordering Mexican counties, and even arrest/deportation rates. Another great comparison would be to include the copycat policies (e.g. Alabama, Indiana) to test for the different effects. Immigration policy is essential to continuously research, as it connects to a myriad of subjects and affects the lives of many. With the help of research and data, policy implementation may be appropriately used for the benefit of the people.

---

11 This goes in hand with the human capital theory, as many born-raised citizens are considered skilled workers, due to their educational attainment and prior job history (Chassamboulli & Peri, 2015).

12 Many individuals were forced, as they had left their families and children behind. In addition, they needed funds and resources, as they are scarce (Sanchez, 2017).

WORKS CITED

Acemoglu, D., & Pischke, J.-S. (1999). Beyond Becker: Training in Imperfect Labour Markets. *The Economic Journal, 109*(453), F112–F142.

Amuedo-Dorantes, C., & Lozano, F. (2015). On the effectiveness of SB1070 in Arizona. *Economic Inquiry, 53*(1), 335-351.

Azoulay, P., Jones, B. F., Kim, J. D., & Miranda, J. (2022). Immigration and Entrepreneurship in the United States. American Economic Review: Insights, *4*(1), 71-88.

Borjas, G. J. (2017). The Earnings of Undocumented Immigrants. NBER Working Papers 23236, National Bureau of Economic Research, Inc.

Chassambouli, A., & Peri, G. (2015). The labor market effects of reducing the number of illegal immigrants. Review of Economic Dynamics*, 18*(4), 792-821.

Edwards, R., & Ortega, F. (2016, November). The Economic Contribution of Unauthorized Workers: An Industry Analysis. *The National Bureau of Economic Research*. Retrieved December 13, 2023, from https://www.nber.org/papers/w22834

Engbom, N. (2022, January). Labor Market Fluidity and Human Capital Accumulation. *National Bureau of Economic Research*. Retrieved December 13, 2023, from https://www.nber.org/papers/w29698

Hoekstra, M., & Orozco-Aleman, S. (2017). Illegal Immigration, State Law, and Deterrence. American Economic Journal: Economic Policy, *9*(2), 228-252.

Looney, A. (2016, July 29). Unemployment and Earnings Losses: A Look at Long-Term Impacts of the Great Recession on American Workers. Brookings

Lundh, R., & Shepperson, A. (2023, November 13). Map the impact: US immigration demographics. Immigration Impact.

Passel, J. S., & Krogstad, J. M. (2023, November 16). What we know about unauthorized immigrants living in the U.S. Pew Research Center.

Peri, G. (2014, May). Do immigrant workers depress the wages of native workers? IZA World of Labor, Institute of Labor Economics (IZA), 1-42.

Piyapromdee, S. (2021). The Impact of Immigration on Wages, Internal Migration, and Welfare. The Review of Economic Studies*, 88*(1), 406–453.

Ruggles, S., Flood, S., Sobek, M., Backman, D., Chen, A., Cooper, G., Richards, S., Rogers, R., & Schouweiler, M. (2023). IPUMS USA: Version 14.0 [dataset]. Minneapolis, MN: IPUMS.

Sadowski-Smith, C., & Li, W. (2016). Return Migration and the Profiling of Non-Citizens: Highly Skilled BRIC Migrants in the Mexico–US Borderlands and Arizona's SB 1070. Population, Space and Place, 22(6), 487–500.

Sánchez, G. E. (2017). The short-term response of the Hispanic noncitizen population to anti-illegal immigration legislation: The case of Arizona SB 1070. Journal of Economics, Finance and Administrative Science, 22(42), 25-36.

Valdez, C. R., Lewis Valentine, J., & Padilla, B. (2013). "Why we stay": Immigrants' motivations for remaining in communities impacted by anti-immigration policy. Cultural Diversity and Ethnic Minority Psychology, 19(3), 279-287.

Wallace, S. J. (2014). Papers Please: State-Level Anti-Immigrant Legislation in the Wake of Arizona's SB 1070. Political Science Quarterly, 129, 261-291.

Wang, C. (2023, February 27). What's Next for Arizona's SB 1070 and Other Copycat Laws. American Civil Liberties Union.

The Impacts of COVID-19 on Education Inequality in America:
A Statewide Study of 2017-2022

By **Lauren Perez**
Sponsored by **Mary Kaltenberg, Ph.D.**
Economics, New York

ABSTRACT

In this study, the impacts of COVID-19 on already prominent education inequality in America is studied. This research covers all 50 states as well as Washington DC from the period 2017 to 2022. SAT scores are used as the dependent variable as they are a measure of academic performance. As the United States switched to remote instruction during COVID-19, education inequality exacerbated as broadband access was not available for students at an equal level. Access to resources has already been inequitable for lower socioeconomic and minority groups, causing a large divide within education. Therefore, within this study, the main variable of interest was internet subscriptions as a percentage of total households. This variable was interacted with a series of time dummy variables to see the effects of internet access on SAT scores within specific time periods, i.e., COVID. Other variables include, logged income, unemployment rate, the Gini coefficient, percent of individuals below poverty, white population, black population, Asian population, and Hispanic population, and percent of students who took the SAT. Within the study, a baseline model, a fixed effects model, and a weighted least squares model to adjust for heteroskedasticity, were all used. The results showed that COVID-19 did widen the inequality gap between lower income and minority students. It is important that the United States works to correct this divide through policy implementation, or the country will experience significant decline in Gross Domestic Product in the future.

INTRODUCTION

The history of the United States is one of systemic inequality throughout almost every system. Education is not an exception to this idea, but rather, is one of the main catalysts for persistent inequalities throughout one's lifetime. Inequality that begins with education harms the academic pursuits of students that will follow them for years to come. One of the main contributors to education inequality is a lack of equitable access to resources in different areas throughout the country. Students from lower income and more rural areas experience more resource shortages than students in more affluent areas. Additionally, non-white students are more likely to experience vast inequality.

When the COVID-19 pandemic forced schools to shift from in-person learning to remote instruction, this inequality exacerbated and the gaps between different socioeconomic and racial groups widened (Agostenelli et al., 2020). Within this research, the degree of this widening was investigated. By using SAT scores as a measure of academic performance, the years 2017 to 2022 were studied to examine the impacts of COVID-19 on education inequality in America on a statewide basis. The period of 2017 to 2019 was used as a period "before COVID," and the period 2020 to 2022 was designated as "during COVID." It is hypothesized that COVID-19 furthered education inequality throughout the United States because the vital resource of remote learning, the internet, was not available at the same rate for all people. It was less likely that students that came from lower income households had access to the internet compared to more affluent, white students. This broadband divide is hypothesized to have contributed to increasing levels of inequality in American education.

While this research contributes to a new subject of research on COVID-19 in recent history, its understanding is incredibly vital to the nation's economic future. The decrease in academic performance across America has contributed to decreasing human capital which will decline the skilled labor force, harming Gross Domestic Product (GDP) for years to come. In addition, this decline will affect different groups of people at different rates, contributing to further inequality throughout the United States.

LITERATURE REVIEW

Inequality within education is not a product of COVID-19. The United States has one of the most unequal education systems in the world, with minority and low-income students being the most affected. The most economically disadvantaged districts usually have the largest population of minority and low-income students concentrated throughout the area, which begins to show the gap between different groups. One of the reasons for this gap is that funding is unequal for instructional methods, such as different technologies (Darling-Hammond, 2001). The gaps that already existed in education became highlighted during the pandemic, making it consequential to research. Uncovering the disproportionate effects will allow policy makers to implement the necessary legislation to make up for the academic losses experienced during COVID.

Remote learning was a lackluster alternative for in-person schooling. In previous research, analysts used empirical research to show that students from poorer neighborhoods were worse off during this time. They discovered that students from these areas lacked access to resources, including parental attention. The research showed that students from lower-income homes were more likely to have parents that were essential workers during the pandemic, and therefore were unable to work from home and invest time in their children's schooling. It has been discovered that children living in poorer neighborhoods experienced a .6 standard deviation loss in learning, measured through GPA and test scores (Agostenelli et al., 2020). This decline in human capital will result in a decrease of job opportunity later in life as today's economy has less demand for unskilled labor.

The socioeconomic and racial divide within remote learning was furthered through unequal access to broadband. Broadband infrastructure is often absent in rural areas and internet is often unaffordable in urban centers, especially among minority families. Only 57 percent of adults that had an income below 30 thousand dollars had access to broadband during the pandemic. Additionally, a 10-point increase in economic disadvantage within a rural area leads to an 18 percent decrease in the ability for teachers to hold classes remotely. In urban areas, with large populations of minority students, a 10-point increase in economic disadvantage led to a 23 percent decrease in the likelihood of holding virtual classes (Patrick et al., 2021). These statistics show an obvious divide within socioeconomic and racial groups. Without being able to hold class because students do not have access to internet, it can be hypothesized that their academic performance levels will decrease, leading to an increase in education inequality.

An additional study conducted in 2021 furthered the understanding of the issue surrounding the inaccessibility of broadband. The study collected survey data from American families from April 2020 to May 2021 to examine how much access American households had to internet resources and how accessibility changed over time. That study's authors also used the data to discover the gaps between different groups within the study. They found that 85 percent of households had access to the internet at the beginning of the pandemic. As schools began to acclimate to the new reality of remote learning by October 2020, almost 95 percent of people had access to internet and computers. However, there were large differences in access for different demographic groups based on race and income. The results show that among those surveyed, only 67 percent of those that make under 25 thousand dollars reported having access to internet or computers. This is comparable to the 97 percent of families that make over 150 thousand dollars that reported having access. Additional findings in the research show that black families were also less likely to have access to technology. This shows the widening gap between socioeconomic groups and race that was already prominent throughout the education system, which furthers the hypothesis of increasing education inequality throughout COVID (Haderlein et al., 2021).

Despite the improvement in internet access throughout the pandemic, simply having access is not enough for the ability to follow along in remote schooling. Reliable internet is just as crucial, if not more to the learning experience. Black and Hispanic students were more likely than white students to receive internet devices from their schools. However, this did not eliminate the digital divide as 13.4 percent and 13 percent of black and Hispanic students, respectively, still did not have access. Although students were able to obtain access to devices, these devices were not reliable as they could not perform all tasks that were required for remote learning such as video chats. Reliable access significantly impacted time devoted to learning. A study collected data from the US Census Household Pulse Survey which asked families how many hours their children spent with their parents, teachers, and by themselves on remote learning for the previous seven days. Black students with reliable access, spent 2.5 more hours than white students studying alone or with parents. Hispanic students spent 3 more hours learning with parents than white students, and 5 more hours studying alone (Francis and Weller, 2023). This study gives relevant insight into an often unobservable characteristic: motivation. However, despite the motivation, not having critical access to resources still furthers the hypothesis that inequality gaps widened throughout COVID.

Despite the motivation of students with reliable access, performance levels dropped on all levels. A study from June 2022 used testing data from 5.4 million students across the country over the first two years of the pandemic. They discovered that math achievement decreased by .20 to .27 standard deviations and reading decreased by .09 to .18 standard deviations. However, this decline was disproportionate which is seen through the increase of the achievement gap among low and high poverty schools which grew .10 to .20 standard deviations (Kuhfeld et al., 2022).

A study from 2023 seeking results on the same topic, found that the main reasons for the divide was due to broadband access as well as differences in engagement levels. The study used percentage of students that qualify for free lunches as a measure of low and high poverty schools. It was found that those from lower levels of poverty had an 85.5 percent level of engagement versus those who were from higher-poverty schools who had a 79.2 percent level of engagement (Gee et al., 2023). Low engagement levels in education severely impact the ability to perform at a necessary academic level. This suggests that students fell behind in their academic pursuits. However, the difference in engagement levels between low poverty and high poverty schools suggest that inequality is increasing throughout the system.

School closures during COVID-19 have already had severe economic impacts. Due to school closures, many non-essential working parents ultimately decided to quit their jobs to focus on their children, which distorted labor market participation throughout the country. A study done by NBER showed that both men and women experienced declines in labor force participation, but the decline impacted women more. Women were more likely to take the role of caretaker while their children were out of school. Therefore, the female labor market may not go back to pre-pandemic levels for years to come (Garcia & Cowan, 2022). Additionally, a 2020 study done by the Institute of Labor Economics has projected that learning loss for students during COVID may lead to up to a 2.6 percent decline in lifetime earnings, leading to a poorer quality of life for today's students (Psacharopoulos et al., 2020).

SET-UP

The theory of education inequality has always existed, even before COVID-19 plagued the United States. However, this research sought to examine if COVID-19 had a further impact on this inequality, specifically an impact on the already existing socioeconomic and racial divide within education. SAT scores were used as the dependent variable as a measure of academic performance. However, an important note must be made that when using SAT scores. There may be significant selection bias, as not all people are required to take the SAT. Therefore, the variable "Took SAT" is included within the SAT to control for this possible selection bias. SAT scores still give a measure of academic performance, as it is a universal exam taken by people in all 51 state entities being studied. To observe a possible socioeconomic divide, the Gini coefficient, percentage of people below poverty, logged income, and the unemployment rate were included in the study. The Gini coefficient fits into the category of socioeconomic divide as it is a measure of income inequality. The Gini coefficient ranges from zero to one. Zero indicates "perfect equality" i.e., everyone receives an equal share of income distribution. One indicates "perfect inequality" i.e., where only one group or one individual gets all the income distribution within an area. For the purposes of this study, it is hypothesized that the closer to one a state's Gini coefficient is, the larger the decline in SAT scores will be during COVID. Additionally, it is hypothesized that larger numbers of individuals below poverty would lead to larger declines in SAT scores. The unemployment rate during COVID-19 increased drastically, putting the United States in a recession after two consecutive periods of economic decline. During this recessionary period, American families were struggling financially, leading to larger declines in income and higher rates of poverty. Therefore, more students struggled than before as their families faced economic hardship. It can be hypothesized that a higher unemployment rate will have a negative effect on SAT scores.

The education divides in the United States are not only specific to socioeconomic factors. Different race groups experience different levels of education inequality. Within this study, variables of white non-Hispanic, black non-Hispanic, Asian non-Hispanic, and Hispanic populations were controlled for. According to the previously mentioned literature, the most affected students during COVID were minority students, specifically black and Hispanic students (Haderlin et al., 2021). Therefore, this study hypothesizes that those populations will see the largest decline in SAT scores in the given period.

This hypothesis looks at the theory of supply and demand for internet subscriptions and devices throughout the pandemic. When schools shut down, the demand for the Internet skyrocketed. However, due to a lack of preparation and guidance from the federal government, school districts and state governments were not adequately prepared to meet this growing demand with an equal supply. This shows that there was a "shortage" of broadband access throughout the country. However, the previous hypothesis can be applied to broadband access as well, meaning that the shortage of broadband access impacted the academic performance of lower income groups and non-white races to a larger degree. To measure the inequality within broadband access, the variables internet subscription and access to one or more computing devices have been added to this research. Since the research surrounds the impacts of COVID-19, internet subscriptions are interacted with a series of time dummy variables to examine the differences in broadband during the given period and if there was an obvious divide during COVID-19. It is hypothesized that during COVID, this interaction will show a decline in SAT scores because research shows that in-person learning is much more effective than remote instruction.

This study consists of three different economic models, a baseline model, a fixed effects model that includes control variables, and a weighted least squares regression.

METHODOLOGY

This study was conducted on a statewide basis, that included all 50 states and the District of Columbia over the period 2017 to 2022. The year 2017 was chosen to increase variation across the sample. All data was collected from the Census Bureau's American Community Survey where all race variables, internet subscriptions, and the Gini coefficient were sourced from. Median income and unemployment rate were retrieved from The Federal Reserve Bank of St. Louis (FRED), and SAT scores and percentage of students who took the SAT were obtained from the United States Department of Education. The summary statistics are presented below:

Summary Statistics

	mean	Sd	Min	Max	p25	p75
Score	1110.42	90.11	936	1298	1047	1195
Internet Subscriptions	33.475	2.63	26.94	45.25	31.83	35.24
Unemployment Rate	4.64	1.79	2.2	13.5	3.4	5.5
White non-Hispanic (%)	71.019	14.20	22.16	93.98	62.43	81.64
Black non-Hispanic (%)	12.33	10.47	.557	47.75	4.30	15.94
Asian non-Hispanic (%)	3.88	5.44	.043	38.69	1.44	4.55
Hispanic (%)	13.248	10.57	1.587	50.15	5.79	16.30
Gini Coefficient	.4690	.020	.4225	.5305	.456	.4804
Income	76,567.	13,119	48,610	108,900	67,030	86630
Log Income	11.23	.173	10.79	11.60	11.11	11.37
Individuals Below Poverty	.1238	.027	.0701	.193	.1025	.1388
Took SAT	43.88	35.97	1	100	4	73
N	271					

Table 1 reflects a summary statistic.[1] All variables were calculated on a statewide basis from all 50 states and the District of Columbia, from the period 2017 to 2022. SAT scores were obtained from the United States Department of Education, and they were calculated as state averages from each year's senior high school class. Internet subscriptions were obtained from the Census Bureau's American Community Survey which obtains surveys from every household that responds. Within this study, it was calculated as a percent per total households per state. The unemployment rate was obtained from the FRED and is seasonally adjusted. Race variables were also obtained from the American Community Survey, and they are calculated within this research as a percentage of total population per state. The Gini coefficient was obtained from the Census Bureau and is calculated on a scale of zero to one, with zero being "perfect equality" and one being "perfect inequality." Additionally, income was obtained from FRED and was calculated as median per state. Lastly, individuals below poverty were retrieved from the Census Bureau. For this research, it was calculated as a percentage of the total population per state.

Within this data, there were missing values within the Hispanic population variable. There were 31 missing values within the variable across the six-year period. Besides the Hispanic variable, the data had complete coverage across the study. The caveats that arise from the sample presented is that

---

1 A summary statistic provides a summary of large datasets to better understand trends within the data. Each variable in the study is included in a summary statistic. The categories of the table include the mean of each variable, the standard deviation, the minimum and maximum values of each variable, the 25th and 75th percentiles of each variable.

there is potential for a larger variation within the study through studying district levels, which can be done in future research. Additionally, since the American Community Survey has some unresponsiveness, there could be measurement error within the state samples.

The data presented was placed into three different models: a baseline regression, a fixed effects regression, and a Weighted Least Squares (WLS) regression. The models are presented below.

Baseline:

$$SAT\ Scores_t = SAT\ Scores_{st} = \beta_0 + \beta_1 Internet_{st} + \beta_2 \sum_{j=t}^{5} \theta_j\ (Internet_{st} * t)$$

The baseline regression[2] includes the main variable of interest, internet subscription, as a percentage, interacted with a series of time dummy variables to differentiate for different years in the given period. The is not included as this is a fixed effects regression.

Fixed effects regression with controls:

$$SAT\ Scores_{st} = \beta_0 + \beta_1 Internet_{st} + \beta_2 \sum_{j=t}^{5} \theta_j\ (Internet_{st} * t) + \beta_3\ lnincome_{st} + \beta_4 unemployment_{st}$$

$$+ \beta_5 Gini_{st} + \beta_6 \sum_{r=i}^{3} \beta_r race_{st} + \beta_7 \sum_{k=s}^{50} \beta_k state_{ks} + \beta_8 \sum_{j=t}^{5} \gamma_j year_{jt} + \mu_{it}$$

The fixed effects regression presented above has a lin-lin functional form[3] and includes all variables presented in the model. Z is a vector of controls of race variables. The race variables included within it are white-non-Hispanic, black non-Hispanic, Asian non-Hispanic, and Hispanic. Income was logged within the model to make its interpretation easier within the model.[4] Since these variables are calculated over time, a fixed effects model was used. Within a fixed effects model, time variant variables are controlled for. The explanatory variables presented in the model are also correlated with one another leading to further evidence for fixed effects being the appropriate model type. Fixed effects can also remove the biasedness that is included in unobservable characteristics that can be found within the error term. Since this study has the limitation of omitted variable bias because it is difficult to quantify relevant factors such as ambition and motivation during COVID-19, fixed effects is the most appropriate model to use. However, heteroskedasticity is often found within the error term when using a fixed effects model. Therefore, to

---

2 A baseline regression includes only the main variables of interest, in this case internet subscriptions per household in percent form and a series of time dummies.
3 Lin-lin functional form presents both the independent and dependent variables in their original unit form as both experience a constant change.
4 When a variable is logged, it becomes interpretable in percentage form. With variables that have large quantities, such as income, it is easier to understand and analyze it as a percent rather than its regular linear, dollar, form.

robust the standard errors and control for heteroskedasticity, a weighted least squares regression was run, which is presented below:

$$SAT\ Scores_{st} = \beta_0 + \beta_1 Internet_{st} + \beta_2 \sum_{j=t}^{5} \theta_j\ (Internet_{st} * t) + \beta_3\ lnincome_{st} + \beta_4 unemployment_{st}$$

$$+ \beta_5 Gini_{st} + \beta_6 \sum_{r=i}^{3} \beta_r race_{st} + \beta_7 \sum_{k=s}^{50} \beta_k state_{ks} + \beta_8 \sum_{j=t}^{5} \gamma_j year_{jt} + \mu_{it}$$

A weighted least squares regression was most appropriate for this study as it deals with statewide level data. Within statewide data, there exists heteroskedasticity due to the variation and differences of attributes within each state throughout the country. This variation can have an impact on the accuracy of the model, due to the possible misestimation of the standard errors, leading to inaccurate t-statistics which effects the significance levels of the variables. Therefore, a weighted least square model applies a weight onto a variable to correct the standard errors within the model. In this specific weighted least squares regression, the weight was applied to population. From there, that weight was applied to each variable as it can be argued that the differences in population density impacts the other independent variables in the model.

RESULTS

After establishing the dataset used from various sources, understanding the appropriate functional form, and creating the models presented above, the three different regressions were run. The results of the study are presented in the Table 2 on page 116.

Within the results table shown, the base year is 2017.[5] It is important to point out that in 2020, during the peak of COVID, SAT scores declined by 110 points overall when not differentiating between races and socioeconomic groups, which is shown in the coefficient in the fixed effects regression in the column denoted as 2020. This shows that the United States' academic performance declined immensely during COVID-19. The coeffect is also significant at the .01 level, meaning that it is a credible result. As aforementioned, a Weighted Least Square model adjusts for heteroskedasticity which is vital in a statewide study where significant variance is present. Adjusting for heteroskedasticity creates a more accurate model. The year 2020 in the WLS model shows that the magnitude SAT scores decreased by 151 points, signifying an even larger, more reliable decrease in academic performance during covid. These coeefficients show that the overall academic performance among all groups of students in 2020, the peak of COVID-19, decreased. However, the rest of the variables within these models show how this decrease was

---

5 All years are compared to 2017 as it is the base year.

Regression Results

	Dependent variable: Score		
	Baseline	Fixed Effects	WLS
	(1)	(2)	(3)
factor(Year)2018	19.840	-12.320	-32.580
	(78.190)	(55.170)	(50.400)
factor(Year)2019	-31.380	-77.280	-84.970
	(78.600)	(58.060)	(52.680)
factor(Year)2020	-40.710	-110.100*	-151.900***
	(79.930)	(57.010)	(52.440)
factor(Year)2021	-54.950	11.860	-16.170
	(82.080)	(59.370)	(50.670)
factor(Year)2022	0.949	14.540	-24.950
	(80.400)	(57.170)	(49.550)
Internet	-2.664	1.130	-0.223
	(2.857)	(2.366)	(2.039)
Logged Income		36.860	16.520
		(29.400)	(27.390)
White Population (%)		0.520	0.426
		(0.400)	(0.428)
Black Population (%)		-7.148*	-9.549***
		(3.755)	(3.215)
Asian Population (%)		0.143	-0.310
		(0.518)	(0.430)
Hispanic Population (%)		-12.800**	-14.790***
		(5.498)	(5.397)
Unemployment Rate		2.639*	2.284
		(1.550)	(1.398)
Below Poverty (%)		-0.0001**	-0.0001*
		(0.00003)	(0.00004)
Gini		-36.660	9.685
		(242.300)	(201.800)
Took SAT (%)		-1.745***	-1.795***
		(0.108)	(0.112)
	(2.429)	(1.721)	(1.564)
factor(Year)2019:Internet	0.655	2.277	2.586
	(2.408)	(1.767)	(1.598)
factor(Year)2020:Internet	0.525	2.634	4.001**
	(2.465)	(1.753)	(1.601)
factor(Year)2021:Internet	1.731	-0.959	-0.090
	(2.416)	(1.727)	(1.487)
factor(Year)2022:Internet	-0.239	-0.949	0.281
	(2.358)	(1.652)	(1.443)
Observations	306	271	271
R^2	0.166	0.668	0.663
Adjusted R^2	-0.043	0.552	0.545
F Statistic	4.413*** (df = 11; 244)	20.160*** (df = 20; 200)	22.080*** (df = 20; 200)
Note:			*p<0.1; **p<0.05; ***p<0.01

Table 2 shows the results of each regression that was run in this study. The models used above include a baseline model, fixed effects model, and a weighted least square model. Each of these regressions show slightly different results as they each have different properties in how they are calculated. However, they each contribute meaningful results within this study to explain how COVID-19 exacerbated education inequality in the United States.

inequitable among non-white students and those that come from a lower socioeconomic status.

The main variable of interest, internet subscriptions, has a coefficient of -2.664 in the baseline model. The coefficient shows that for every percent increase in internet subscriptions per household, SAT scores decrease by .0027. While this goes against the initial hypothesis, there can be a logical explanation for the negative relationship between these two variables. Even though internet is a crucial tool for the educational process, having access does not imply that it will be specifically used for academic purposes. Access could have led to less academic productivity for students which led to lower outcomes in academic performance. When the other control variables were added in the fixed effects and weighted least squares, the variable became more negative, which is expected when more variables are added to any model.

A series of dummy variables was created to specify between access to internet subscriptions during COVID and non-COVID years. The year 2017 was dropped for the purposes of perfect collinearity.[6] The overall trend between the years studied is a positive one, showing that if students had access to internet subscriptions, SAT scores increased. The year 2020 shows the largest magnitude of effect, specifically when it is adjusted for heteroskedasticity in the weighted least squares regression. Within the WLS model the coefficient is significant and shows that in 2020, if the student had access to internet, then SAT scores increased by .004 points. The coefficient is also significant at the .01 level. The significance of the 2020 coefficient is relevant to this research because 2020 was the beginning as well as the peak of the COVID pandemic. In 2020, almost all students were learning remotely as COVID rates were skyrocketing and there was little mitigation. Therefore, students that did not have access to internet were at a disadvantage in academia. In 2021, the trend turned negative again within the fixed effects and WLS models. This trend could have been due to students returning to in-person instruction in several states, so internet was not as vital. While only the WLS coefficient in 2020

---

6 Perfect collinearity occurs when one or more variable within the dataset is a "copy" of another variable. When perfect collinearity exists in a model, it becomes unsolvable, so it must be corrected for.

is significant individually, the F-statistics[7] for all models are statistically significant at the .01 level.

In the model, the income was logged, creating a lin-log relationship between the two variables. Income was logged as it deals with large quantities and is more interpretable and more easily analyzed in logged form. When a variable is logged, it is interpreted in percent form. Within the fixed effects regression model, the coefficient shows that for every percent increase in income, SAT scores increase by .3686 points. The positive coefficient shows that there is a positive relationship between income and SAT scores. If income increases, SAT scores do as well. This proves an integral part of the hypothesis that more affluent students have more academic success. When logged income is presented in the WLS regression, the magnitude of effect decreases, but it still shows a positive relationship that when income increases by one percent, SAT scores increase by .16 points.

The results for race variables are also presented within the table. Since the race variables are calculated as a percentage of total population, the coefficients are divided by 100. For the percentage of white population, the coefficient shows that for every percent increase in the white population, SAT scores increase by .005 points. When looking at the WLS regression, for every percent increase in the white population, SAT scores increase by .0046 points. While the magnitude of these coefficients is small, the positive relationship is relevant. The positive relationship shows that white students had increasing SAT scores.

The other three non-white races, Asian, Black, and Hispanic, show a negative relationship between population and score. The models show that the Hispanic and Black Non-Hispanic populations saw the largest decline of SAT scores. In the fixed effects model a one percent increase in the black population led to a decline of .7148 points. The coefficient is significant at the .01 level, meaning that there is reason to believe that this statistic is accurate. The WLS coefficient shows that a one percentage increase in the black population led to .095 decline in SAT scores. This coefficient is significant at the .05 level which is an even larger significant level, furthering the credibility of the result.

The Hispanic population also had significant, negative results. The decline for the Hispanic population was higher than that of the black population. In the fixed effects model, as Hispanic population increased by one percent, SAT scores declined by .128 points. When adjusted for weighted least squares, the magnitude of effect gets larger and gains significance.

---

7 F-statistical testing is used to test the significance of two variables when they are combined to create what is known as an interaction. Here, internet is combined with time because time-period is vital in a COVID-19 study when in 2020, internet usage was much more necessary in academic settings.

As Hispanic population increases by one percentage point, SAT scores decrease by .1479 points, which is significant on the .01 level. These variables show a disproportionate impact in education on different racial groups, with white students being the only population to experience a positive trend with SAT scores.

Unemployment rate signifies that for every point increase, SAT scores increase by 2.639 points. This result is significant at the .01 level and indicates a positive relationship between SAT scores and the unemployment rate, which is different from the initial hypothesis. The literature review presented above describes a possible explanation for this. When parents were home, they potentially paid more attention to their children and their academic success. Therefore, when a parent was unemployed, SAT scores increased because they were more focused on their children's education (Agostenelli et al., 2020). In the WLS model, the coefficient loses significance but still has a positive relationship with SAT scores.

When looking at the percentage below poverty, the fixed effects regression states that for every percent increase in the number of individuals below poverty, SAT scores decrease by .000001 points. The coefficient is significant at the .05 level. When the WLS model is observed the coefficient remains the same but loses significance as it becomes significant at the .01 level. The magnitude of effect is incredibly small, but the negative relationship is relevant as it shows that those below poverty had worse outcomes in academic performance during COVID-19.

While the magnitude of effect is extremely small among percent of individuals below poverty, the Gini coefficient gives a larger insight into inequality. The coefficient shows that for every point increase in the Gini coefficient, SAT scores decline by 36.6 points. This supports the hypothesis. The decline in SAT scores shows the magnitude of that inequality. In more unequal areas, SAT scores declined significantly. However, when adjusted for heteroskedasticity, the WLS model shows that for every point increase in the Gini coefficient, SAT scores increase by 9.68. While this goes against the initial hypothesis, it can be logical. The nation became more unequal during COVID as a whole because of large rates of unemployment. However, as aforementioned, unemployment led to parents being able to pay more attention to their children and their schoolwork, potentially improving their academic performance (Agostenelli et al., 2020).

Finally, it must be noted that there is omitted variable bias within this study due to the selection bias within the SAT. Not all students take the SAT, and during COVID more colleges were waiving the SAT. Additionally, students were not enrolling in colleges, so fewer people were taking the SAT (Di & Caldwell, 2022). Therefore, a variable of the percentage of people that took the SAT was included in the model. As percent of people who took the SAT increases, scores decrease by .0017 points. This is an expected trend because as more people take the SAT, there's a larger pool of people that will do poorly.

DISCUSSION

From the results presented above, a clear divide between socioeconomic and race groups was discovered. The coefficients of income and race give insight to the divide that was originally hypothesized. A one percent of income leads to a positive increase in SAT scores, approximately .374 points. When this is corrected for heteroskedasticity, there is an even larger magnitude of effect, with a coefficient of .5815 showing that for every percent increase in income, SAT scores increase by .5815 points. The significance as well as the magnitude of effect regarding logged income shows that there is a divide between different socioeconomic groups, where those with a larger income far outperform those with lower percentages of income. Additionally, regarding race variables, the hypothesis was proven correct that different race groups saw larger declines in SAT scores, while white students saw an increase in SAT scores. All non-white races included in the model saw a decline in SAT scores over the given period, except Asian students within the fixed effects model. However, even though Asian students experienced an increase in scores within the fixed effects model, the magnitude of the coefficient was smaller than that of white students. A one percent increase in the Asian population led to a .0010 increase in SAT scores, as opposed to a .00475 increase in scores for white students. It was discovered that the black and Hispanic population experienced the largest decline in SAT scores, which follows the trend of previous research (Haderlin et al., 2021). The differentiation in academic performance can be attributed to a lack of access to internet for remote instruction. While the coefficient alone is negative, when it is interacted with year dummy variables, it shows during the period of COVID, SAT scores saw an overall trend of increasing SAT scores if the student had access to internet. Therefore, students with less access to internet were worse off during the pandemic, leading to a substantial decline in SAT scores for minority communities and lower socioeconomic groups.

The results of this research prove a clear divide in the United States education system, and COVID-19 exacerbated the situation to a larger degree. A study for the University of Pennsylvania used forecasting model techniques to predict that if this decline persists, the United States could lose enough of the skilled labor force that by the year 2050, GDP will decline by 1.4 percent (Paulson, 2021) This staggering statistic shows the potential for an extreme loss of this county's economy, and the global economy as well which can lead to financial and economic ruin for future generations. Education is the starting point for all people. An unequal education system will lead to an unequal future for students.

Using the results of this study as well as previous literature, policy implementation is necessary to improve the outcomes and reverse the probable future outcomes due to the decline in education during COVID. A possible policy that can be implemented is the investment in universal broadband, especially in underserved communities. For decades, the United States has thrown money into the education system. While there has been some improvement in the system over the years, too many students are still being left behind. Therefore, investing in internet itself and working towards implementing cell towers in rural communities, can make a large difference in the educational outcomes of all students. Additionally, subsidizing internet providers to implement broadband in these communities can make the idea more attractive to them which can lead to them lowering the cost of their services to these communities.

While the study presented sets a solid foundation for the overall impacts of COVID-19 on education divides within the United States, previous research can go into more detail. In the future, district level analysis would help to pinpoint more details about rural versus urban communities in the United States and how region effects access to broadband and overall scores. Additionally, using a different examination, such as eighth grade state level exams, can lead to an even more insightful analysis. By the time students can take the SAT, they can mostly be trusted to study and learn without as much assistance that younger students may need. Therefore, looking at eighth graders or younger can provide a deeper analysis of the education divide throughout America during the pandemic. A study of younger students will possibly show an even larger divide than the one presented here.

CONCLUSION

Education is an integral part of the growth and development of an economy. A good education can lead to better economic outcomes for all people within a nation. However, since the education system is inherently unequal, it leads to inequality for generations to come. The COVID-19 pandemic only exacerbated this situation to a further degree. What usually was a lack of resources within schools became a lack of resources within student's homes, severely impacting outcomes. To ensure equality in the education system, policy implementation surrounding broadband is crucial. A prosperous education leads to a prosperous future for the United States and the world. The United States should prioritize its students and ensure that all students, regardless of income or race, receives the same equitable access to resources, especially internet resources in a growing technological society.

WORKS CITED

Agostenelli , F., Doepke, M., Sorrenti, G., & Zilliboti , F. (2020, December). *When the Great Equalizer Shuts Down - National Bureau of Economic Research.* www.nber.org. https://www.nber.org/system/files/working_papers/w28264/w28264.pdf

Burkholder, E. W., & Salehi, S. (2023, May 11). *Effects of the COVID-19 pandemic on academic preparation and performance: A complex picture of equity.* Frontiers. https://www.frontiersin.org/articles/10.3389/feduc.2023.1126441/full

Darling-Hammond, L. (2001b). *Inequality in Teaching and Schooling: How Opportunity is Rationed to Students of Color in America.* Inequality in Teaching and Schooling: How Opportunity Is Rationed to Students of Color in America, The Right Thing to Do, The Smart Thing to Do: Enhancing Diversity in the Health Professions -- Summary of the Symposium on Diversity in Health Professions in Honor of Herbert W. Nickens, M.D., The National Academies Press. https://nap.nationalacademies.org/read/10186/chapter/9#209

Di, W., & Caldwell, M. (2022). *Students cut college during pandemic; their return is uncertain.* Federal Reserve Bank of Dallas. https://www.dallasfed.org/research/swe/2022/swe2201/swe2201b

Francis, D. V., & Weller, C. E. (2022, March 1). *Economic Inequality, the Digital Divide, and Remote Learning During COVID-19.* www.journals.sagepub.com. https://journals.sagepub.com/doi/full/10.1177/00346446211017797

Garcia, K. S. D., & Cowan, B. W. (2022, January 17). *The impact of U.S. school closures on labor market outcomes during the COVID-19 pandemic.* NBER. https://www.nber.org/papers/w29641#:~:text=Our%20results%20show%20that%20both,likely%20to%20work%20at%20all

Gee, K. A., Asmundson, V., & Veng, T. (2023, July 11). *Educational impacts of the COVID-19 pandemic in the United States: Inequities by race, ethnicity, and socioeconomic status.* Current Opinion in Psychology. https://www.sciencedirect.com/science/article/pii/S2352250X2300088X?ref=pdf_download&fr=RR-2&rr=81cd6cfc0ac741df

Haderlein, S. K., Saavedra, A. R., Polikoff, M. S., Silver, D., Rapaport, A., & Garland, M. (2021). Disparities in educational access in the time of covid: Evidence from a Nationally Representative Panel of American families. *AERA Open, 7.* https://doi.org/10.1177/23328584211041350

Kuhfeld, M., Soland, J., & Lewis, K. (2022, June 30). *Test score patterns across three COVID-19-Impacted school years.* www.journals.sagepub.com. https://journals.sagepub.com/doi/10.3102/0013189X221109178

Mazrekaj, D., & Witte, K. D. (2023, July 10). *The impact of school closures on learning and mental ... - sage journals.* journals.sage.com. https://journals.sagepub.com/doi/abs/10.1177/17456916231181108

Patrick, S. K., Grissom, J. A., Woods, S. C., & Newsome, U. W. (2021, December). *Broadband Access, district policy, and student ... - sage journals.* journals.sage.com. https://journals.sagepub.com/doi/10.1177/23328584211064298

Paulson, M. (2021, October 27). *Covid-19 learning loss: Long-Run Macroeconomic Effects Update.* Penn Wharton Budget Model. https://budgetmodel.wharton.upenn.edu/issues/2021/10/27/covid-19-learning-loss-long-run-macro-effects

Psacharopoulos, G., Collis, V., Partrinos, H. A., & Vegas, E. (2020, February 2). *Lost wages: The covid-19 cost of school closures.* IZA Discussion Papers. https://docs.iza.org/dp13641.pdf

The twenty-fifth volume of *Transactions*
was published in Spring 2025
by Pace University Press

Cover and Interior Layouts by Zetta Whiting and Kayleigh Woltal
The journal was typeset in Verdana and Georgia
and printed by Lightning Source in La Vergne, Tennessee

Pace University Press

Director: Manuela Soares
Faculty Advisor: Eileen Kreit
Production Consultant: Joseph Caserto
Graduate Assistants: Zetta Whiting and Kayleigh Woltal
Student Aide: Liz Abrams

9 781965 246023